I0769844

WE NEED
REAL DEMOCRACY

O. Iakovidis

TABLE OF CONTENTS

PREFACE
(some author's words)

Humans are "tuned" by Divine Nature, to seek intentionally or uninten-
tionally happiness throughout their Life journey. That is, to feel pleasure.
- For "what offers pleasure to humans", there have been volu-
  mes of philosophical thoughts referring the main human
  pleasure which, at the same time, promotes society.

And this, is no other, than the conquest of Freedom, individual and
social. Therefore, this pleasure should, above all, seek humans not only
as individuals but also as a society.

- Humans are two-sides beings.

They have physical and spiritual substance (body and spirit) that one
constantly fights the other; the joy that many times take from the
satisfaction of one, oppresses and disturbs the other.

- Humans are social beings.

They can't live out of society. One could even say that every human
being is an infinitely small piece as one out of the billions of cells that all
together create the great and immortal human creation, which is the
human society.

- Considering these unquestionable Truths, we are obliged to feel,
  as free Humans are compelled to contribute, with any power at
  their disposal, to resistance against any effort for imposing
  another "order" that is opposed to the "nature of things" that offers
  deep pleasure to every one of them.

- Man can't care only for himself and his flesh. He cannot just be a shit-machine. As mentioned above, he is, by his very nature, social, as it is impossible to live outside a group/society.
- Thus, each person has to offer to the group/society even the slightest, his sole will if nothing more, for improving the well being of his belonging group/society.

The agonizing yell of the great thinker and writer Nikos Kazantzakis, who puts his hero on to exclaim *"I have the duty to save the world all by myself. If it is not saved, I'll be guilty",* it comes to "bind" with the ancient admonitions of old and new intellectuals that show to every citizen his debt to society, which starts from debt to himself and his family.

This debt, which is a debt to Freedom, I see it very clearly now, walking towards the twilight of life, free from the daily hunting of livelihood, which, usually, with the pressure of every day's life, prevents the contemplation of the "big picture".

Perhaps (as a "non-academic") I'm not legitimized to present and put to the public debate positions and views on a huge political issue, such as the insidious assault that the Democracy takes on all the widths and lengths of the Earth from its eternal enemies, the Oligarchy and the Monarchy.

But, I think I'm fully legitimate, having acquired the status of an active citizen who, for the last ten years, has served both, from the position of the free political columnist (with hundreds of articles on the Internet) and from the position of the political activist, I've been taken by excellent fighters but (and above all) next to the prominent figure of the great Greek visionary and global democrat, the composer Mikis Theodorakis.

I had the honor to be chosen between his close and trusted associates during the development of the "SPITHA" Movement of Independent Citizens. The last political attempt that this great Greek and Democrat attempted to overthrow the barbaric regime, which is presented as Democracy and has handed over the Greek society to its cynical lenders/oppressors, signing shameful "Memorandums" of submission.

I'm legitimate also because I'm a citizen who has never had any party involvement in ruling regime, which is now proven to be the perfect tool for the society's enslavement.

I'm legitimate as I find that my sovereign state (the Greek, but not only) systematically, for decades, not only leaves society uneducated about what Democracy is, but (and this is the worst) falsely distorts Truth and hide under its disguise as Democracy, a two-headed Oligarchy (Political and Economic).
It governs the State, apparently now, as an agent of offshore powers (those of "lenders"). Forces that are totally aligned with the obvious aspirations of the "International Empire of Money", which, in its impeccably modeled globalization, show how the new international, stateless and transnational "Empire of Money," with religious characteristics, is being formed, having as its prophet "Consumption" and using as its temples, the Banks. .
In fact, according to my experience, I consider Greece, during this period (2010-2017), as a field of cutting-edge political experimentation, for the uninhibited imposition of the will of the "International Empire of Money" in societies belonging to the arc of the "Representative Democracy ".

Finally, I am legitimate by the fact that, by moving towards my personal "final exit", I don't aim (with the wording and disclosure of my thoughts) to gain personal benefits.
Guided by the need to pay my debt to Freedom and Democracy, I give my last personal battle to what is worth millions of such battles: of the (real) Democracy, which is the only safe road to the happiness of human society, and to the elevation it brings to human existence.

In the giant global propaganda that aims to establish a barbarous Oligarchy, which is presented (too sneaky and persuasive) as Democracy, I stand upright like David against Goliath, having armed my sling with an unbeatable weapon: the Truth !!!

My prayer: This sling, to become a small "Bible of Democracy" that will help the everyday fighters of the (real) Democracy to illuminate with the light of Truth, so to break the darkness of the ruling Oligarchy's big lies.

The structure of this small "Bible of Democracy" helps this end.

I wish you, dear reader, through a PLEASANT READING, to open a window on the horizons of the tomorrow's society, as FREE PEOPLE want, free from "right" or "left" obsessions.
And I hope that some readers of this manual will become active preachers of its Truth.

I, myself, have already earned my profit.

It is the personal deep pleasure of taking part in a big, difficult but nice fight.
The struggle of
Logic against dogmatism,
Truth against lies,
Freedom against enslavement,
Democracy against Oligarchy,
Light against darkness,
Good against evil.

Othon Iakovidis
(Thessaloniki / Greece, Sept. 2017)

INTRODUCTION

"You can have either FREEDOM or QUIETNESS.
Both, together, don't coexist.
You have to choose:
Either you'll be FREE, OR QUIET "

"Conspiracy theories"

Many people, when listening to or reading something that overturns the knowledge we have on a specific subject, especially when it's a political or economic issue, think (and it's reasonable to think so) that what we hear or read is a proof of some "conspiracy" that the rivals of our solid knowledge, know.

It's logical, however, to think that it can't be excluded, the subversive views we hear or read, to be true.

It would be best to read (or listen) in a strictly critical spirit (but without empathy and firm dogmatism) any subversive (of our knowledge) version, in order to reject it.
But if the subversive version is not discardable but it's based on solid arguments and tangible evidence, then we should, if not immediately adopt the new view, seriously reflect upon our faith in our established knowledge that we had before.

- I'd encourage the readers of this manual, to read it in this critical way.

Someone, of course, could ask:
- Why should I be interested? Is it more important than finding a job, or a love mate, or planning my summer break, listening to a music that I like or going to see an interesting play in theater or a film in cinema?

- Why should I've to spend my time for reading about the Democracy"s need (according to the writer's aspect)?

The answer to this question is given by the **Great Plato** (427-347 BC) who, by his masterful metaphorical "CAVE" urges since then:
No one is more enslaved than those who erroneously believe they are free.

So, my dear reader, if you have understood what Liberty and Democracy means and you are aware of the value of your personal freedom and the freedom of the society in which you live, you ought not only to dedicate your time to read about the protection of the highest values of Freedom and Democracy, but dedicate far more than your time, to be activated for prevention of any attempt for enslavement of your society, which leads directly to your personal enslavement.

Let you feel, the nice and great pleasure of participating, in a nice, difficult struggle, for brave ones.

The excellent highbrow Cornelius Castoriadis, writes:
"We need this constant creative activity of the public and this means, above all, the passion for the public.
If there is no such passion for the common, we can say good speeches, we can write fine books, construct systems that are impeccable, philosophical and political, but they will not mean anything" *if they'll not become specific acts.*

There are crimes and crimes. Minor or bigger, out of negligence or passion, premeditated or by accident, forgiven or inexcusable.
This book deals with one very large crime, perhaps the largest that is repeatedly going (over the last 150-200 years) against the mankind.

This crime is the uterus of millions other crimes that are carried out daily in human society, with hundreds dead, and tons of untold suffering, on a personal level, on a family or national level.

We are talking about the (premeditated) murder of Democracy !!!
That's to say the murder of the principles who raised the human being
from the stage of "thing" ("res") which was sold and purchased in the
Agora/Market, and made him a "citizen", that is, a person entitled to
decide himself on the way of his living in society and in his State.

It is, of course, worthy of attention that the way in which this long-term
killing is done by application of the Mithridatism* method. That is to
say, in order the crime of Democracy's reprisal not to be perceived,
this is attempted by granting to the organization (in small instalments,
continuously increasing appropriately) the deadly poison of the atony
(until their complete abolition) of the basic constituents of the
Democracy. Equity in speaking, equality in front of the Law, equality
on Political Rights (as documented in this manual).

The reason why those seeking the Democracy's killing, want their
attempt not to be perceived, results from the analysis of the subject in
the following chapters, where is analyzed this great crime and
documents the traces that identify the culprits.

There is also (at the end) a proposal for how society can bring the real
Democracy back to its small communities as well as to the large
States, but also to a "Globalized Real Democracy".
This proposal is a radical political concept that can take mankind
away from the hell of war, refugee, hunger, poverty, environmental
despair.

- * Mithridatism. For those who don't know the story,
  Mithridates was King of the Pontus (Black Sea State) who
  lived in the 1st century AD; he, fearing the possibility of
  poisoning him, acquired immunity to poison by taking small
  doses of venom, ever increasing. Since then, "Mithridatism"
  is called, through addiction, a practice of self-protection by
  the action of a poison.

AND AN INTRODUCTORY NOTE:

- Whatever is mentioned in this manual that it is happening in
  Greece, most of the times and in most cases, are not just
  about Greece.

- What happens in a "Democratic Country" (like Greece) is very
  likely to be happen in any other.

SYNOPSIS

Typically, the synopsis of a treatise is written at the end of it, as a conclusion of all the previous ones.
Let me change this established position and put here, as a first chapter, an hypothetical (but realistic) dialogue that could be the summary of all the next chapters.
Thus, the following chapters are the analysis and documentation of this "summary's" contents

---

How and why the Oligarchy decided to be presented as Democracy.

(I was not an eyewitness, but the realism of the below fantastic dialogue , is derived from the measurable economic and social results recorded in the societies of "Representative Republics" globally).

According to the historical evolution of the human society as described in the relevant chapter (HISTORICAL ROUTE OF DEMOCRACY), the hypothetical dialogue developed below is suitable for the time when the Monarchy (in the 18th century AD) understood that, in order to save a part of the absolute sovereignty she had so far on society, she was obliged to share this sovereignty with the emerging (then) political and economic elite of that time, creating ever since, the ubiquitous ruling Oligarchy .

When Plato described in his "Cave": ***No one is more enslaved by those who erroneously believe that they are free*** (about 400 BC), he may not have imagined that some (seeking their power over an enslaved society) would use it, two thousand years later, thinking about as follows:

- Don't we want society, fully enslaved?

- Nice !! Let's do what Plato says: So let's convince society that it's free, and so it will be submissive to our own decisions and interests. (He, the smart one of the company, thought).

- How can this happen? (asked, again, the Monarchy)

- (the smart of the group, had studied the subject. He took the floor and began his speech):

- It is enough for our Oligarchy to be "passed" as Democracy, whose concept is identical to Freedom and Self-determination, which every citizen, all over the world, wishes with all his heart, ready to sacrifice himself for these ideas !!! ...

- And to do this, it's enough to "tease" (so smooth that it can't be easily understood) the core of the Democracy: we will settle as People's decision, the decision of surrogate persons who will (or will easily) be ours.

- These persons will be legalized and authorized (from "Democratic" Constitutions that our own jurists will compile) to represent the people, so that their decisions can legitimately be decisions of the State, on any matter concerning its people.

- In fact, these persons (the People's representatives) will be elected by elections from the People so that the Democratic element of the "deciding majority" to have existed in the election of those persons who, whoever they are, will be (or will become) ours, meaning they will defend our interests.

- And because the involvement of few people is easier than the involvement of many, the "representatives" of the People, it's good to be grouped into some, few, groups with a common characteristic of these groups: obedience of their members to the leadership of each group.

- If any such group (let's name it "party", after its fragmenting the whole part of the People's body) will appear to represent the interests of a social class, the better for the development of competitiveness among the parties. The rivalry will help to better conceal the truth, that behind each such party (irrespective of its "ideological positions") we will be the ones who (by presumption) will have "captured" its leadership.

- To ensure that the leadership of the ruling parties will be (always) obedience to us, we must take great care and ensure that we always have the mechanism of political propaganda in our hands. With the proper dissemination of messages acting as psychotropic substances, this is what will act as a mechanism for manipulating the people's thoughts and will lead (to a large extent) the People, in our choices.

- The mass media ownership by us, will be ensured, by belonging only to us.. The safest safeguarding is when the media ownership is accessible only by large portfolios, which, presumably, belong to our elite.

That's all ! In this simple way, we will achieve the complete enslavement of society, since it will believe it is free.

- Hey Plato! with your wisdom, you opened our eyes ....

From the way in which the political practice in all the States that operates the "Representative" or "Parliamentary" "Republic", as well as the results recorded for two centuries now in the societies of these States, it seems (little or much) that with this reasoning was constructed and organized the Oligarchy as "Representative" or "Parliamentary" "Republic".

Since then, it has been functioning flawlessly in most societies of the world, named as "Democracy". (How does the propaganda's mechanism work so that the society can be convinced that it decides for its fate while others decide, is developed in the relevant chapter "DEMOCRACY AND MASS MEDIA")

The following chapters are a complete documentation of this fantastic but absolutely realistic narrative.
The "Representative Republic" is not Democracy.
It is a formal Oligarchy, disguised and self-presented as Democracy.

And, let's not forget: whoever is disguised is trying to cheat ...

IS DEMOCRACY
THE BEST POLITICAL SYSTEM ?

Churchill on Democracy:
«None pretends that democracy is perfect or all-wise. Indeed, it has been said that Democracy is the worst form of government except all those other forms that have been tried from time to time».

———

If we haven't a DOCUMENTED ANSWER to this question, there is no point in thinking about whether we should or should not support Democracy.

- The view that YES, DEMOCRACY IS THE BEST POLITICAL SYSTEM is documented by the following:

Human society is an extremely complex living organism.
In order to work smoothly, organization and rules are needed.
Its fundamental organization must provide for:

- 1. Who decides for what has to be done (on every problem in society)

- 2. Who carries out the decisions made

According to what Aristotle has written and from the experience of 2,500 years of governing human societies on all the widths and lengths of the Earth, we can say that three (and only these, with the versions of each) are the Political Systems that any society can have:

(A) MONARCHY, in which the decisions concerning the life of society are taken by the Monarch.

- He, (with the appropriate instruments of his own, which he appoints and controls) decides and carries out these decisions on every issue that concerns society.

(B) OLIGARCHY, in which decisions concerning the life of society are taken by a small leadership group. It (with the appropriate organs of its own, which it appoints and controls) decides and carries out these decisions on every issue that concerns society.

(C) DEMOCRACY in which the decisions concerning the life of society are taken by the whole of its People. It (with the appropriate instruments of its own, which it appoints and controls) decides and carries out these decisions on every issue that concerns society.

- None of these three Political Systems can coexist with one of the other two, since the hard core of each ("who is deciding" according to his interests) is in contrast to the hard core of each of the other two .

- Not having, then, the possibility of some sort of synthesis among these three political systems, we should look at which of the three is best for human and his society.

And, when we say "best polity," we mean the political system that helps to achieve a "good living" of human / citizen within his state.

That is, a life that offers joy. And, the life of human gives him joy when his basic material and spiritual needs are covered, regardless of his personal potential.

The basic material needs are: food, clothing, housing, health-care, traffic, security.

- Covering these needs requires money. (As much as necessary for the best coverage of these needs).

- The basic spiritual nature needs are the feelings of every citizen:

    1. about the existence of Justice,

    2. for his value as a citizen, that it is not less than anyone else,

    3. for free access to his education, which is not minor of anyone else,

    4. about his potential for creative employment, according to his ability and talent

    5. for his information of good quality

    6. for his leisure,

    7. for his philosophical or religious contemplation, without exclusions,

    8. about the everyone's ability to improve his standard of living,

    9. for his social recognition.

For covering these needs, freedom is required.

Which political system can better meet these (material and spiritual) needs of citizens?

- The answer is self-evident: That one, which gives more freedom and more money to meet these needs.

Let's see which one of the three Political Systems can give more.

MONARCHY (in which the Monarch doesn't account to anyone) has NO OBLIGATION to benefit the People upon which he is governing. Monarch, he will do what he considers necessary, according to his own opinion, needs and interests, without asking the society that exists to serve his needs.

OLIGARCHY, is no different from the Monarchy, in dealing with the society. It's the same. The society exists to serve the Oligarchy's needs.

In **DEMOCRACY** (the real one) in which (as we've seen) the decisions concerning the society's life are taken by the entire community, it is self-evident that these (material and spiritual) needs are fully and foremost covered.

So: The Political system, which can best cover (material and spiritual) needs of society, so that every citizen can have a pleasant (if not happy) life, is Democracy.

And of course, this is not an original conclusion.

Human societies, on all the widths and lengths of the Earth, have been filled with rivers of blood and millions of dead, cripple persons and refugees, for paying this choice.

On the contrary, no popular Movement or Revolution, was made, ever, for the dominance of the Oligarchy or Monarchy.

- But, we must not overtake the **Oligarchy that tries to be convincingly presented as Democracy** (as is the case with "Representative Republic").

"REPRESENTATIVE REPUBLIC", in order to convince the society that it is not a variant of Oligarchy but is a kind of Democracy, is forced to make benefits not only of an economic nature but also in the field of Civil Liberties for meeting the society's spiritual needs.

Of course, these benefits (both of them) reach to the limit that doesn't harm the interests of Oligarchy, which are summarized in three main points:

- In storing of wealth in the hands of the Economic elite (which is the one pillar of the Oligarchy)

- In maintaining political power in the hands of the political parties elite (which is the second pillar of the Oligarchy).

- In maintaining the possession of the propaganda mechanism in the hands of the Oligarchy.

The propaganda mechanism consists of "circular education" and the Mass Media (MM).

- Circular Education is running by the Political elite, the MM are managed (almost all) by the Economic elite.

Whatever overcome these basic needs of the Oligarchy, it goes to meet the above mentioned needs of society.

This distribution of "pie" in all the "Representative Republic" world, is evidenced by the fact that, for 150-200 years, there is a continuation of wealth hoard in the account of the economic elite, (local and international) along with the deprivation of much of society.

DEMOCRACY IN ANCIENT ATHENS

All the world admits that the Democracy was born in Greece, and indeed in ancient Athens, in the 5th century BC.
Its birth didn't happen suddenly, overnight.
It was a result of a long maturing of political thought on the field of philosophy on one hand and the maturing of social conditions evolving at that time in Greece on the other.
(Korn. Kastoriadis "... *it is no coincidence that its birth coincides in a very substantial way with the birth of this unlimited questions over questions that philosophy consists of"*).

We are talking about the period beginning in the 7th century BC and ending in the 5th century BC.
Very briefly, things (in terms of the Political evolution) developed as follows:

The Political System that existed in Athens at the time of its foundation, the Bronze Age and the peak of the Minoan civilization (2,500-1,500 BC), was Monarchy and the hereditary transfer of power from father to son.
The King, as a mediator between men and God, was the absolute master over all living beings and inanimate objects that existed in his kingdom.

The Athenian Kingdom (Monarchy), along with this divine relationship and continuity, was interrupted by the tyrant Dragon. Thus, Tyranny (also Monarchy) is, historical, the first form of political power that challenged the Kingship along with Gods' will.

On 624 BC, the "institutions makers" ("THESMOTHETAE" in Greek) instructed the wise citizen Dragon to draft new legislation, which was also the first written law of ancient Athens.

In 621 BC, Dragon recorded for the first time his rigorous laws ("Dragon aconite laws") on marble slabs, which were in common sight, at the city marketplace.

Dragon's laws were maintained for only thirty years because they were particularly tough.

For those years, the power belonged to the leaders of large landowning families who had the power to impose the law according to their interests, through a system of harsh Oligarchy.

The injustice that gave birth to this system in society brought the functioning of society into "suffocation", and the philosopher **Solon** was called to arbitrate and find the solution.

Among other measures, he applied "SEISACHTHEA", which abolished the right of the lenders to take slaves, due to debts, the borrowers and the members of their families; he, also, canceled the debts of the individuals to each other and to the State.

The Political system that prevailed in Athens for the next 30 years, with election of the "well-known Lords", was ARISTOCRACY, namely Oligarchy.

The period of Aristocracy was terminated in 560 BC, when Peisistratus, who established Tyranny, took over power. He was succeeded by his sons Hippias and Hipparchus, who were the last tyrants (Monarchs) of Athens.

After the fall of this Tyranny (in 510 BC), **Cleisthenes** proceeded with very important reforms and laid the foundations for transforming the regime of Athens into Democracy.

An important part of the power passed onto the citizens and all of them, regardless of social order and income class, had the right to participate in the "making decisions" process.

Nevertheless, the axioms in the hierarchy of power were distributed according to the economic situation of each citizen.

The economic class of every Athenian citizen determined his taxation and thus his political rights.

The more he paid in taxes, the greater the privileges he enjoyed. That is, the possessors of welth were also the leading class of the State.
The classes, according to their income, were four.
The inferior economic class had no right to stand for election but to vote.

According to Cleisthenes' reforms, citizens of the 2nd and 3rd class gained the right to become members of the "PARLIAMENT OF 500", which previously composed only from 1st economic class citizens.
The institutions of the State, after the reforms of Cleisthenes, were:

1. The CONGRESS OF THE PEOPLE ("ekklisia tou dimou", in Greek), established by Solon in 594 BC.

- This was THE MAIN DEMOCRATIC ASSEMBLY IN ANCIENT ATHENS, and was held on the hill of Pnyx, or on the Marketplace or on the Theater of Dionysus, near Acropolis.

- The assembly was open to all male citizens who had political rights and were older than 18 years of age.

- They were deciding by majority vote on every issue concerning the City's issues.

2. THE "PARLIAMENT OF THE 500"
- The Parliament of the 500, the most populous body of officials, was the organizing committee of the CONGRESS OF PEOPLE preparing legislative drafts and defining the themes of its meetings.

- From 487 BC the 500 deputies were appointed by yearly lottery.

- A citizen could be member of the PARLIAMENT OF THE 500 no more than two times.

- Every citizen could make suggestions to the Parliament.

- Every day of the year one of the deputies was the head of the state for this day. For example, he held the keys of the treasury and the seal of the State, and was responsible for the reception of foreign missions and, during the 5th century, chaired the parliament and the "CONGRESS OF PEOPLE".

It has been estimated that about a quarter of all citizens should have held public axioms sometime in their lives. This position of somehow "head of state" could be held by everyone during lifetime.

Political Parties did not exist.

3. "AREOS PAGOS" was the Supreme Court in ancient Athens.

- It belonged to the so-called "murderous" Courts because of the cases it was holding. It was responsible for murders or fatal injuries.

- Members of this Court were the outgoing "nine Lords" of the Athenian State.

4. ELEA was the main court of the ancient Athenian State.

- This was a court of jury, members of whom could have been all original Athenian citizens over 30, after a draw.

- Hiring someone in ELEA did not require any special education, but having to do with legislative work resulted in a fairly good knowledge of the laws. The ELEA consisted of 6,000 judges ("Eleastes"), who were coming from the 10 Tribes of Athens, each Tribe participating with 600 members.

- The Lord of Court gathered the complaints and the cases to be heard and determined by lot the section and place where the case would be brought.

- As there were no lawyers, the defendants asserted their own defense with the help of a single friend or relative. Many times, they were commissioned to write a speech about their case assigning this task to a professional writer. The time of speaking was limited by a hydraulic timer, the hour-glass.

- The vote was secret. In the event of a tie, the accused was Innocent; they believed he had "the vote of the goddess Athena".

As we can see as a general rule of thumb, the basis of Democracy in ancient Athens was the control of every citizen by the whole community, as well as the control of the community by each citizen.

From 479 BC, in contrast to Cleisthenes' reforms, a peculiar oligarchy is established in Athens, as the members of the Supreme Court (AREOS PAGOS) took over, by overcoming the established principles.

This peculiar and anachronistic junta created strong disagreements, dividing the Athenians into "Oligarchs" and "Democrats," without this division to receive any sort of party's shape.

At that time there was a political reform in Athens made by Ephialtes of Sophonidou (not to be confused with Ephialtes who betrayed Leonidas in Thermopylae).
Ephialtes, as leader of the "Democrats" movement, accused the noble Areopagites for mismanagement and the "CONGRESS OF PEOPLE" voted their referral to the Court of ELEA.
 Penalties for the areopagites who were found guilty were devastating.

With this reform, many privileges have been removed from the Areios Pagos and were transferred to the "CONGRESS OF PEOPLE", to THE PARLIAMENT OF 500 and to the ELEA.

After liberation from the yoke that Areios Pagos had imposed, the developments were constant and rapid.
A basic one was the equal participation of all citizens to all public axioms (except for the axiom of "Lord General" which was similar to nowadays President or Prime Minister) since in the predominant view of the ancient Athenians and Greeks in general, democracy did not require any special knowledge, as politics was not perceived as a science but as an area of opinion where all those who are concerned with it have an equal right of speech and participation in decision-making.

With these changes brought about by the interventions from Ephialtes of Sofonides, the system became fully democratic.

From 461 BC, Pericles, who was elected continuously for 14 years (until his death) as "Lord General" of Athenians Democracy", dominates the political life of the city.

The thirty years that followed until the outbreak of the "Peloponnesian War", was a period of great prosperity for Athens and became known as "Pericles' golden age".
Pericles strengthened further the democratic nature of the government by taking a series of prolific measures.

NOTE: What we notice in Athens, about 700-400 BC. and then on, is the constant change of institutions. The political institutions were never ideal. Though the Athenians never ceased to reform their laws in such a way so as to increase the reality of Democracy, namely the possibility of real participation of People in power.

DEMOCRACY'S COLLAPSE

Democracy in ancient Athens was constantly challenged by the Oligarchy of wealthy families. It finally collapsed, after the diplomatic and military victories of Macedonian Philip II and his son Alexander the Great, in order to unite all the Greek Citiy-States to a force against the persistent enemies of Hellenism, the Persians.

Since then, Democracy as a Political System was completely disappeared from Greece and the rest of the world.

DEMOCRACY'S HISTORICAL ROUTE UP TO NOW

Democracy, after its collapse in ancient Athens, has been disappeared for centuries not to be found as the Political System of a city or a State either in Greece or everywhere on Earth.

The Monarchy of the Macedonian Empire of Alexander the Great and his successors (extending for about 2 centuries: 330 BC to 30 BC) was succeeded by the Roman Empire. Throughout 27 BC to 476 AD, was weaving between Monarchy, which the Emperors sought, and Oligarchy, which the noblemen/landowners were desperately trying to enforce.

The thousand-year-old Byzantine Empire (Eastern Roman Empire), which reached up to 1453 AD, when Constantinople fell into Turkish hands, was a field of action exclusively for the Monarchs.

The same happened with the Ottoman Empire, which succeeded Byzantine and reached the 20th century. It was also, purely Monarchic.

Throughout the Middle Ages and from the 5th century AD to the 15th century AD, the different tribes (Goths, Franks, Germans, Slavs, Saxons, etc.) were organized in Europe with principles purely monarchic.
A notable fact is that in 1295, England, was the first country in Europe to acquire a parliament by taking a first step from Monarchy to Oligarchy.

With the Renaissance (14th-17th centuries AD) in Europe, when the spirit of ancient Greek philosophy begins to diffuse into societies, people are beginning to demand more and more Freedom.
In trade-developing societies (Venice, Florence) we see the oligarchy developing at the expense of Monarchy.

The American Revolution (1757) was made at the request of the US Independence from England, of which it was a protectorate. By gaining their independence, the United States acquire a Constitution that establishes a "Representative (Presidential) Republic".

The French Revolution (1789) was born by the demand for Democracy and succeeded so. However, France soon ended up into becoming a Monarchy (Empire of Napoleon).

The Greek Revolution (1821) was a struggle for liberation from the yoke of the Ottoman Empire. The first Constitution (1827) of the liberated Country is "Representative Democracy", but soon Monarchy is imposed by the European Kings. King of the Greek State became a Bavarian Prince (Otto).

German Tribes united (about 1815) under Monarchical powers and formed the precursor of today's Germany, which becomes a State in 1871 named the "German Empire" – (Monarchy).

At the same time, Slavic tribes took shape and form the Kingdoms of Russia, Bulgaria, Serbia, all of them constituting Monarchies.

The Italian city-States, that were created after the collapse of the Roman Empire (all of them organized as Monarchies/Kingdoms), are united, in 1871, and create the Italian State. Its' name was "Kingdom of Italy" and it is a Monarchy, as well.

In Latin America, at the beginning of the 18th century, societies revolted by calling for their Independence from their European colonial dynasties. Thus, under the Oligarchic or Monarchic regime, the present States were created: Argentina, Brazil, Chile, Venezuela, Uruguay, Paraguay, etc.

In Asia, the big Empires of China, India, Japan, Philippines, Korea, Iran, Arabs and the others, were all, up to that time, Monarchies.

From the 18th century AD, humanity enters the era of "Industrial Revolution" that changed the form of society. The development of industrial production, which boosted the development of Trade and Banking, creates new jobs and new vigorous social classes.

Until then, we find none society in Europe, Asia, Africa and America to be governed by Democracy. Not even by Oligarchy.
Everywhere reigns the Monarchy.

The pressure that industrialists, traders and bankers exert on the workers, as well as the pressure of the big landowners in the newly established US on their slaves, gives men and women the opportunity to grasp the great values of their Freedom and Self-determination.

This fact, in the United States, results to the civil war of North against the South. In Europe, the Monarchs are forced to avoid situations such as the French Revolution of 1789. They grant political privileges to the elites of large landowners, industrialists, traders and bankers, who bloom with the growth of trade brought by the Industrial Revolution.

In Russia of Tsars, the situation escapes the control of Tsar's Monarchy. He doesn't follow the example of other European Monarchies, and the great Popular Revolution of 1917, which establishes a "dictatorship of the proletariat", prevails.

Therefore, we may say with certainty that the Industrial Revolution is the catalyst that forced the universally established Monarchy to deliver much of its power to Oligarchy.
This became possible through the founding of political parties. Since then, Oligarchy established and controlled a political mechanism, in order to manage the political situation. This mechanism is no other than the "Representative Republic".

An important political event is the attempt by the Soviet Union, to implement a system of "People's Democracy", created by the popular revolution of 1917. Though, it had no relation to Democracy what so ever. We mean with the real one, as we have defined it in the chapter " WHAT DEMOCRACY IS ".

The system imposed by the one and only legitimate party developed into an Oligarchy of the party's members. As a result, it collapses by its own in 1999, after 72 years of efforts to stabilize and internationalize it.

Since then, the political situation, in general, is shaped so that in all these societies that are governed by "Representative Republic" actually governs the binary Oligarchy of the Political and Economic elite. This elite of Each country is directly linked, through international, political and economic organizations, to the International Political and Economic Elite.

Weaving the interests of the Economic Elite with those of the Political Elite, a globalized Oligarchy, self-presented as Democracy, has been created. A very well structured and organized elite either within each Country and State or internationally.
Of course, many readers will say that in many Countries/States there is Democracy, as the "Representative Republic" is established in them.
But, is Democracy the so-called "Representative Republic?

The answer is given to the homonymous chapter.

———————————

This rapid review of the Democracy's history throughout the world, shows that human societies have been governed by Monarchies, since the dawn of history.
Nowadays, they've ended up to be governed mostly by Oligarchy and Monarchy, with a single and short interruption by Democracy (for about 140 years), 25 centuries ago, in a single City-State, the ancient Athens, in Greece.

As a result, we can say with certainty that human society has not progressed and has remained almost stationary in the field of its Political development, while technologically it has been jumping.

———————————

WHAT DEMOCRACY IS

The word "Democracy" is probably the most popular Greek word in the world.
This is because, its concept is identical to Freedom, Self-decision, Self-determination, in the consciousness of every human being who uses it.
These are concepts that have become ideals and sacrifice worthy for millions of people to all lengths and widths around the Earth.
And it is due to this heavy content and symbolism that has undergone this ruthless pillage by all sorts of "Democrats" and "Republicans".

"Any African Corporal with ten machine-guns and twenty jeeps take up power and proclaims that he has established Democracy", Cornelius Castoriadis complains in a relative excerpt of his speech (1997).

And, I am adding: 95% of the today's States have in their official terminology of their Political system, the words "Democracy" or "Republic", which means the same for the most of the people.

These two words hide behind them cruel personal dictatorships such as:

- North Korea's Kim Jong Oun

- "Dictatorships of the proletariat", such as the Chinese or the former Soviet Union

- Obscure and insidious Oligarchies such as all the "Representative Republics".

So, a big blur of what is and what is not Democracy has been created probably on purpose.

Democracy, we need to know, is not what each one thinks of.

Democracy is a specific Political System, which operates speicifically.

So, we must name things with their true and original names.

We will attempt here to clear this fog that prevents us from clearly seeing the "correct way" we want to go if we believe that Democracy is the best Political system.

- "Correct way" cannot be anything other than the one that offers joy to a human being on his way of life in human society.

First of all, we need to have a definition of "What is Democracy".

It's necessary not to allow anyone to present a notion on WHAT DEMOCRACY IS according to his/her opinion.

This definition cannot be anything other than the concept of the two Greek (ancient) words (DEMOS + KRATO) which consist and form the word "Democracy", and strictly contextualize its meaning.

- DEMOS (ΔΗΜΟΣ in Greek), is "all the citizens who constitute the Society of a village, city, province, State or Country".

- CRATO (ΚΡΑΤΩ in Greek), means "I hold", "I exercise power", "I am the lord of someone or something", "I am the sovereign on someone or something".

- So, DEMOCRACY (ΔΗΜΟΚΡΑΤΙΑ in Greek) means : all together the citizens (as one person) are the sovereign on their society.

- It is also clear (from its references to the ancient Greek literature) that the word "Democracy" refers to the Political system of a State, ie an organized civil society.

Thus, a simple and precise definition of the term "Democracy" is formulated in: **"Democracy is the Political System by which the People becomes the sovereign of the State "**.

- Because sovereign can be only one who is free to decide by his/her own on his/her matters, and

- because there is a clear model of how this sovereign was operated in ancient Athens, during the 5th century BC,

it's necessary, the definition to be completed as follows, in order not to leave any gaps that may become "holes" or "back doors" and change its meaning:

"Democracy, is the Political System by which the absolute and sole sovereign of the State is its People, ie "altogether the citizens as one person" who decides freely, voluntarily and in person, by majority vote, on every issue that concerns his society".

THIS IS A DEFINITION OF DEMOCRACY, WHICH IS FULL AND SIMPLE.

It is worthwhile, perhaps, to see what was the first definition of the Republic. He was given by Herodotus (484 – 410BC) ("Herodotus History", 3, 80):

> ***"Democracy is the political system in which the People is sovereign, the axioms are assigned by draw, and everyone is accountable for the administration of the principle and the decisions are taken jointly".***

- We see that this definition is virtually not far from the definition we gave above.

I feel compelled to comment on two definitions of the Democracy that are disseminated on the Internet.

1. Abraham Lincoln: *"…government of the people, by the people, and for the people."*

   - This definition is absolutely correct, but it is elusive and generic, so it allows "holes" or "back doors" to change its meaning.

2. WIKIPEDIA : *"Democracy : Form of government, where a constitution guarantees basic personal and political rights, fair and free elections, and independent courts of law".*

- Two notices on this definition:

    1. The existence of a Constitution is not an indispensable element of the Democracy, as it is presented by the definition we've seen before in here. The existence of a Constitution depends on the decision that "the whole of its People" will take on this issue. For example, in ancient Athens, there was no Constitution.

    2. This definition refers to "fair and free elections" but it doesn't specify the subject of the elections. (why?)

However, we must know that: if the elections involve the election of People's Delegates, then we don't have Democracy, but Oligarchy. (This is according to Aristotle and all the main political philosophers of the last three centuries)

The vote on (real) Democracy, concerns only the vote on the A or B choice, on every issue that arises, and never on the choice of Representatives. There are no Representatives in real Democracy. The people decide in person, themselves, directly, without representatives.

The only elected by voting person in ancient Athens Democracy, was the "LORD GENERAL" who was the leader of the Armed Forces and the "PUBLIC TREASURER".

Once the definition of "Democracy" has been drawn up, we should also know the following:

In the definition of the Democracy, it is primarily determined that Democracy is a POLITICAL SYSTEM (and nothing else).

The POLITICAL SYSTEM determines where from the political power is originated and the way it is exercised.

So, in more detail, the Political System determines :

1. The way in which decisions are taken on any matter that a society can face. Some of these decisions become Laws.

2. The way in which the decisions taken, are executed.

3. The way in which the execution of the decisions taken is verified.

4. The way in which the offenders of the decisions taken are punished.

Political System has no political content.

- That is, a Democratic State, may decide to adopt any economic system (eg, socialism or liberalism, or whatever else is decided by the majority of society) without this implying that it is more or less Democratic.

   It is enough the decision to be taken democratically, that is, the majority of people voted for it .

- A society can decide for or against legal or illegal immigration. It can decide whether it wants War or Peace. It can decide for or against the socialization of public goods, for every variation of natural sexual behavior, and for anything else, without the content of the decision playing a role on weather the Political System in this Country is or is not Democracy.

   It's enough that the decision has been taken democratically, that is, the majority of people voted for it .

- Some, ignoring what Democracy is, and trying to blame the Democracy of ancient Athenians for not being a real Democracy, point to the existence of slaves and the exploitation of their work by Athenian citizens.

Well, let those who say these things, understand that the existence or absence of slaves in a society has nothing to do with democracy. The issue of man enslaving man is primarily humanitarian.

The slaves did not disappear from the societies of the "West" because of Democracy, but due to the spread of humanism, to which the dissemination of democratic ideas helped.

Thus, the society of a Democracy that has decided to have slaves can be accused of not having humanity but cannot be accused of not having Democracy since its decision was taken democratically, meaning that the majority of its citizens voted for it.

- Cornelius Castoriadis, writes: *"Democracy doesn't mean eg. human rights, or lack of censorship, or elections at any time. All this is good and holy but in a second and third degree of democracy".*

Note:

It is historically established that three (and only those) are the basic Political Systems that anyone State can have, from the beginning of human society up to the end of it:

(A) MONARCHY, in which the decisions concerning the life of society are taken by the master of the state, who is the Monarch.

S/He, decides and carries out these decisions on every issue that concerns society.

(B) OLIGARCHY, in which decisions concerning the life of society are taken by a small leadership group.

- They decide and carry out their decisions on every matter that concerns society.

(C) DEMOCRACY in which the decisions concerning the life of society are taken by the majority of People/Citizens.

- The People decide by vote and carry out these decisions on every issue that concerns society.

In Ancient Athens, the first complete, real Democratic model, decisions on all matters were taking by the majority of the Athenian citizens, by vote, after gathering all of them in a place.

- That is, the citizens of ancient Athens did not elect representatives, to whom they assigned their will to decide on any matter concerning the Athenian society without further asking the society's will (as happens with modern supposedly "Democracy", the so-called "Representative Republic").

- This "little difference" (People voting for those who will vote on their behalf, instead of voting directly for each law or for every problem) is the "species-making" difference of the popular vote that creates a huge distance between Democracy and Oligarchy.

NOTE: Whether it is or it isn't feasible and practical, all citizens to vote for each law or for every problem of their society is thoroughly dealt within other chapters of this manual.

PRECONDITIONS FOR THE EXISTENCE OF DEMOCRACY

In order to, have indeed, real Democracy in a society, it is necessary to exist some preconditions.

The most important ones are:

THE EXISTENCE OF FREE CITIZENS is a prerequisite for existence of Democracy in a State.

- "Free citizens" are citizens who, in addition to their natural freedom, have "Civil Freedoms". That is to say, the freedom to be sufficiently informed about what is happening and to express and co-shape, according to their will, their society's decisions on any issue.

- Democracy without free citizens is impossible to exist. The notion of Democracy is entirely interwoven with the notion of Civil Liberties since it is logically inappropriate to have freedom of will, where the will have ceased to exist (or banned or manipulated).

- In Democracy, the freedom of every citizen, as well as the State's freedom, is not unlimited, that is unaccountable. The freedom of every citizen and citizens group reaches the limits of the freedom of another citizen or another group of citizens.

- The means that set these limits are the laws which the citizens themselves have voted for.

- CAUTION !! FREEDOM IS NOT IMPUNITY. The Impunity, presented in various cases as Freedom, has eroded the concept of Freedom itself.

THE EXISTENCE OF KNOWLEDGE OF "WHAT INDEED IS THE DEMOCRACY"

- In our days, the notion of "Democracy", helped by a propaganda of huge dimensions, has been brutally alienated and misused. Those who want to deceive convincingly, try to persuade the People that he lives in Democracy.

- Proof of this is the abuse of the word "Democracy", by its incorporation with the "Representative Republic" which is a version of Oligarchy and not a kind of Democracy. It even ended up being used by dictatorial regimes.

- North Korea's "Democracy" of Kim Jung On, China's "People's Democracy" or the former Soviet Union, or the "Democracy" of any Latin-American dictator or African coup has nothing to do with Democracy, although they swear on it !

- It is, therefore, an obligation for every citizen to know about "WHAT DEMOCRACY IS ".

- And, unfortunately, s/he will never learn it to School; it is used as a field of political disorientation, with which the Oligarchy aims at the political stupefaction of youth. Of course, the citizen will not learn about real Democracy by the Mass-Media that are property of the governing Oligarchy.

- MM consist a tool for criticism abilities devaluation, as it is documented in the chapter "DEMOCRACY AND MASS ME-DIA".

3. THE EXISTENCE OF:

(a) "ISIGORIA": which means Equality of every citizen in "speaking publicly"

(b) "ISONOMIA": which means Equality of every citizen against the Law

(c) "ISOPOLITIA": which means Equal chances of every citizen for public axioms .

1. In order for Democracy to exist, it is essential that these three conditions of Political Equality, which constitute the three pillars upon which the Democracy is founded, must exist and function properly.

2. Even if one of them is not exemplary and suffers, then, in this society, the Democracy suffers, if it hasn't yet collapsed; and if its citizens haven't realized it, it's certain that they'll realize it a little bit later.

ISIGORIA: It means that all citizens have the right to equally speak, that is, to make their views and thoughts, public.

- Find out whether, in the Country you live, there is a broad public debate, in the mass-media or elsewhere, about whether "The Representative Republic" is or not Democracy, but Oligarchy.

("Broad public debate" means the provision of an approximately equal time (or pages) to that provided in the endless, silly and hollow confrontation between the political parties and their members).

- Get the conclusions yourself.

ISONOMY: It means that all citizens are equal against the Law.

- The equality of all citizens against the Law is carried out with the participation of all for the righteousness of justice. That is, Justice, in order to ensure its decisions correctness, is awarded by courts consisting of citizens selected by draw (such as the jury Courts). And this applies to all areas of justice: criminal, commercial, political, administrative, everything.

- Throughout the "Western world" of "Representative Republic", in order to find your right, you need a "good" (ie expensive) lawyer, which only "the ones who possess", can afford.

- So, we are not all the citizens equal against the Law. Those that "they have", they are more equal from the others that they haven't.

Look if, in the Country you live in, this is true or not.

- Get the conclusions yourself.

ISOPOLITEIA: It also means that all citizens have the right to equal participation:

- (a) in the formulation and implementation of decisions concerning everyone.

- (b) in claiming public axioms, that is, in the distribution of political power.

   If others (and not the citizens themselves, in person) are deciding and the citizens just obey, then these two parties are not equal, as those who are obliged to obey what others have decided are captives of the other's decisions. That is they aren't free since they are captives.

   So, in order to be free, citizens must be political equal.

   That's how political equality becomes Citizens' Freedom.

- In the ancient Athenian Democracy, citizens are appointed by drawing lots on the public axioms (about 700). An exception is the axiom of the "Lord General" and the Public Cashier; for these, a vote was held because they need specific knowledge and skills. They were obliged to obey in the decisions taken by the "House of People's Will" ("EKLESIA TOU DIMOU").

- Throughout the "Western" world of "Representative Democracy," who can claim "equal rights" on getting public axioms? Elections are absolutely under marketing terms that means "whoever spends more he/she will go higher".

- Is that "political equality"?

- Look if, in the Country/State you live in, this is true or not.

- Get the conclusions yourself.

- Ask (and answer to yourself) if you are free or marionette of some liars and crooks and decide what you want to be.

Many of the greatest thinkers and philosophers have concluded about **What Democracy is.**

Some of their thoughts will be mentioned below (as it is written by George Oikonomou, in his "Direct Democracy", p. 69-70):

- **Thomas Hobbes** (17th cen.) De Cive (1642) Fr.transl. Samuel Sorbiere, CF-Flamarion,Paris 1982, ch. VII,1)defines Democracy as the state in which sovereign power belongs to an assembly that everyone has the right to vote, while the Aristocracy (or Oligarchy) as the State in which the power belongs to a council composed of only a few and not by all.

And he adds: in the Democracy governs the People, while in the Aristocracy the nobles or the "important" of the State.

- **John Locke** (17th cen.) "Two Treatises of Government" (1690) trans. "GNOSI"-Athens 1990, ch. X) defines as Democracy the human community in which the majority has all the power to legislate. The majority also appoints officials to enforce the laws. If the majority assigns power to the hands of a few select individuals, then it is the son of Oligarchy. (here Locke clearly gives us the definition of today's "Representative Democracy" as

- **Baruch Spinoza** (17th cen.) "Political Treatise" transl. Pattakis – Athens,1996, ch. 2,17) writes that if the concern for the adoption, interpretation and abolition of the Laws, for the fortification of the cities, for the decision on war or peace, belongs to an assembly consisting of the crowd as a whole, then we have Democracy . If this concern belongs to selected individuals, then it is Aristocracy.

- **Mondesquieou** (18th cen.) The Spirit of Laws, transl. GNOSI-Athens 1994, partI, book II, ch. II) also states that when in a State the body of people has the dominant power, we have Democracy, while when power is in the hands of some people, we have an aristocracy. He points out, moreover, that the draw belongs to the nature of the Democracy while the election to that of the Aristocracy.

- **Jean-Jacques Rousseau** (18th century) "The Social Contract", transl. POLIS, Athens, 2004, book III, ch.3) defines Democracy as the political system in which the government is exercised by all or most of the people in such a way that there are citizens who are lords and not residents. Rousseau also develops the principles of (direct) Democracy in detail, pointing out that the draw matches the nature of Democracy.

- **Hegel** (19th century) considers that Democracy is the political system based on the will of many and how man is forfeited through representation.

The definition of the term "Democracy" and the key points that define WHAT DEMOCRACY IS, as they are written from greatest thinkers and philosophers, will help each citizen to understand better whether democracy exists or not, in his/her country.

ADJECTIVE DETERMINATIONS FOR DEMOCRACY

Many of the real Democracy's supporters use the adjective "DIRECT" to separate it from the other "forms" of Democracy, defined by other adjective determinations, like "People's Democracy", "Liberal Democracy", "Parliamentary Democracy", "Soviet Democracy" and so forth.

- In Wikipedia you can find about 50 different adjective determinations for Democracy !

  When, among others, you can see "Democratic Dictatorship", or "Crowned Democracy" you may understand how serious are all these adjective determinations for Democracy !

  Democracy is only one ; without any adjective determination.

We claim that Democracy is a unique form and nature. It doesn't tolerate any adjective determination, not even the (correct) one of "Direct", because if we'll accept that there is "Direct Democracy", we automatically accept that there's also "Indirect" and maybe (why not?) other forms of Democracy.

Only the use of the adjective "real" is (logically) permitted, as it automatically makes "unreal" any other adjective determination, contrary to the definition "real".

- Thus, a rule is arising: **Any "Democracy", determined by addition of an adjective definition, is not real, ie it's a "Pseudo-Democracy".** (exception to this rule is the "Direct Democracy")

So, annul as Democracy, any kind of Political System which, with any adjective determination, is defined as Democracy.

The use of the adjective definition "real" is judged to be the imperative for anyone who wants to distinguish the real and true Democracy from all the supposedly ones.

———————————

WHAT DEMOCRACY IS NOT

After defining what Democracy is in the previous chapter, let's now look on WHAT IS NOT DEMOCRACY, in order to avoid confusing it.
It's good to know it, and to consolidate it so that we can choose in what political system we want to live: Democracy, Oligarchy or Monarchy.
In any case one of these will be the political system of the society we live in.

1. **It's not a Democracy what is not a Political System.**

- It's reminded that Political System (Polity) is the system that determines where the political power is originated from and how it is exercised.

- Don't confuse the Political System with the Government which is the "Executive Power" in the Political System.

- The other two Powers of the Democracy, are the Legislative Power and the Judicial Power (Judiciary) ...

Thus, socialism, capitalism, communism, liberalism and their derivatives, which are Systems of organizing the Economy of a State, have nothing to do with the concept of the Political System so they have nothing to do with Democracy.

None of them is, by origin, "democratic" or "non-democratic".

The Economic system in a Democracy may be socialistic or capitalistic or whatever other model could be.

- **It is enough that has been decided by the majority of the People.**

Humanism, Patriotism, Internationalism, and every "-ism" that characterizes the various philosophical, religious, cultural theories and trends, have nothing to do with the concept of Political System and Democracy which is one of the three kinds of Political systems (Monarchy, Oligarchy, Democracy) a society can have.

2. It's not Democracy, whatever Political System distorts or opposes the People's sovereignty over the society on which this is exercised.

- That is when the sovereignty of a State/Country proves to be not the majority of its People, but another entity (natural or legal), then it isn't Democracy in this State, no matter how this State/Country is called.

3. **It's not Democracy**, any variation of the concept of "Democracy", that is attempted with the intent of some adjective determination (eg, "Totalitarian Democracy", "Constitutional Republic", "Parliamentary Democracy", "Presidential Democracy ", "Electoral Democracy" etc.).

- None of these variants is (real) "Democracy", since the definition of Democracy (which we must remember) is being circumvented: *"Democracy, is the Political System by which sovereign of the State is its society, ie "all together the citizens as one person" who, decides freely, voluntarily and in person, by majority vote, on every issue concerning its society".*

- About the question, if the so-called "Parliamentary Democracy" or "Representative Republic" is or is not Democracy but Oligarchy, the analysis exists and is developing in the chapter "IS THE REPRESENTATIVE REPUBLIC, DEMOCRACY?"

- The three types of Polity (MONARCHY - OLIGARCHY - DEMOCRACY) cannot interfere with each other for the creation of another mixed type, as the texture of the "hard core" of each one ("who is taking the decisions?") excludes the other two.

  1. This fact cancels, as impossible, the alteration that is attempted with the addition of adjective determinations to the concept of "Democracy".

4. There is not Democracy in a State when the society has a status of impunity.

The one's freedom, stops at the limits that the freedom of the other begins.

Which are these limits, is defined by the (voted by the majority of the People) law.

DEMOCRACY AND CITIZEN

When the first element (DEMOS) of the word "DEMOCRACY" refers to the People, that is to say, all the State's citizens, it is immediately understood that "Citizen" is a fundamental component of the concept "Democracy".

Citizen, in (real) Democracy, is not every human being that happened to be born in a society that wants to be called (and be) Democracy. Citizen, is the human who is interested in life, both his own and his family's, and especially his children, who are (in some way) the continuation of his own life.

The citizen who is interested in his life is the one who constantly tries to be happy of it and enjoy it on the one hand, and on the other hand to improve it.

Through his 5,000 years of history on Earth, man has been taught that a REQUIRED PRECONDITION for a pleasant passage from life is the existence of his Freedom. He has been taught (from history) that the less Freedom he has, the more unhappy he becomes.

Thus, the primary concern of citizen is to ensure his personal freedom.
But it's impossible to have a personal freedom if the society in which he lives is not free.
It's impossible to enjoy and improve his life when the social environment is ill, contaminated, deadly.

So: HUMAN BEING IS OBLIGED to be constantly looking after and trying to have a social environment healthy, clean, pleasant, promising.
This reality causes the citizen to be FIRSTLY interested in his Society's freedom if he doesn't want to lose his own freedom.

This need (to defend the society's freedom in order to secure his personal freedom) made the ancient Greeks consider as "useless" the citizen who was indifferent to the common issues. (Actually, for those citizens they used the ancient Greek word "idiot" which, has the meaning of "the one who cares only about himself").

Freedom, however, doesn't exist in itself, by some Divine Will.
Efforts are needed (sometimes smaller or larger) to exist.
When we don't have it, the efforts to get it are bigger. When we try not to lose it, they're smaller.
However, ALWAYS need efforts to be Free.

The following phrase is given In Thucydides (460-395 BC):
"Freedom and Quietness, they don't coexist. Whether Freedom we'll have, or Quietness. We have to choose".

And of course, in the above dilemma, the surest way to lose our quietness is to lose our Freedom.

So (necessarily) we choose Freedom.
And of course, when we talk about Freedom, within a political narrative like this, we mean Civil Liberties, as the concept of Freedom in general, is enormous and beyond our specific subject.

The Civil Liberties include the following fundamental rights that the citizen has in Democracy:
- The right to participate personally in decision-making on every issue that concerns his / her society.

- The right to free commentary and criticism of decisions on every issue that concerns his society

- The right to participate in the execution of any decision on every issue that concerns his / her society.

- The right to best inform the events concerning his / her society.

- The right to participate in the formation of judgments on all matters concerning his / her society.

- The right to equal treatment of him by the Justice

In (real) Democracy the citizen has and exercises all these rights.
By exercising these rights, the "resident" of a State becomes "citizen".
Democracy is the only Political System in which this change of the resident's status to Citizen (equal to all its other fellow citizens) occurs.
No one has more rights than him. Everyone has equal rights.
Citizen is not every resident.
Citizen is the resident who is actively involved in the daily operation of the political system. Whether as an "MP" or as an executive body, or as a "judge" or as a critic of the system's operation.
And he does it to defend his freedom.
This equality among all citizens in political rights is the fact which guarantees their political freedoms.

This doesn't happen, neither in the Oligarchy, nor, of course, in the Monarchy. Only in (real) Democracy.

The Political System of a State where the citizen is excluded from all or one of these fundamental democratic rights is not Democracy.
And, if it isn't Democracy, then it is Oligarchy or Monarchy, as the mix of polities is impossible (as documented in the chapter "WHAT DEMOCRACY IS").

In the Democracy, all citizens are equal in their civil rights.

- If others are deciding and citizens just obey, then these two parts are not equal, as those who are obliged to obey on what the others have decided are bound from the decisions of the others. Since they are bound they're not free.

That is why political equality is a precondition for Citizens' Freedom.

- If in a decision by the People's will, the vote for the Alpha selection is 55%, the 45% voted for the Beta is not meant as "others", "opposites".
- There isn't "we and the others" in the (real) Democracy because there aren't parties.

Every decision is taken by "us". We (all of us) decided on the Alpha selection.
There are no opponents.
My vote doesn't make me an opponent with those who, on this issue voted differently than me, because in the next vote we'll probably have the same view on the new issue that will emerge.

- And everyone has the right to criticize each decision.

This is the citizen in the (real) Democracy.

And, of course, has nothing to do with the "citizen" of the "Representative Democracy" from whom it has been removed almost all the above rights:

- the right to participate in the decision-making process on every issue of his society has been confined (with parliamentary elections) to the citizen decision on who will decide instead of him.

- That is, his original right has been transformed into a right to assign this right. So, someone else took this right from the citizen and decides on every citizen's issue! Nice !! Isn't it?

- The right to participate in the execution of every decision on every issue that concerns his or her society is trapped; In order to reach public axioms, he/she is obliged to pass through the Party's dark paths.

- The right to best inform the facts about his/her society has been granted exclusively to individuals (the Mass Media owners).

- The right to participate in court decisions on matters relating to his/her society has been delegated to the bureaucracy of the practice of a professional judiciary (judges and lawyers)

- The right to equal treatment by the Justice has been largely lost due to the professional exercise of the legal defense only by lawyers, which creates pay inequalities and consequently inequality in the quality of the legal defense of each case.

- The only right that is allowed to citizen in "Representative Republic" is the right of free commentary and criticism of decisions on every issue that concerns his society. And this, in practice, can be done by a mere audience step that doesn't have the intensity of the public pitch used by the political status that has the Mass Media. With these, the Oligarchy's propaganda, assures daily and convincingly every citizen that he lives in Democracy ...

Let's look at the data over and over and say (to ourselves) if we are free citizens or puppetry, in the "Representative Republic" regime.

And let's decide what kind of citizen we want to be.

Plato's lesson: **None is more enslaved than those who erroneously think they're free.**

]

IS THE REPRESENTATIVE REPUBLIC, DEMOCRACY ?

We'll attempt to answer the question as fully as possible, as it is of interest to hundreds of millions citizens throughout the world.

We'll examine the issue from both sides. Theoretical and practical.

General aspect

Since its appearance and application to the City/State of ancient Athens in the 5th century BC, Democracy was the opposite pole in the dipoles: DEMOCRACY vs MONARCHY and DEMOCRACY vs OLIGARCHY.
Since then, the poles of these dipoles have been in an eternal battle that is underway in our own era, as the Democracy's implementation affects key interests of the Economic Oligarchy, which is one of the two pillars that form the modern "governing Oligarchy" which governs locally (in every "Democratic" Country/ State) as well as internationally.
The other is the Political Oligarchy which consists of the Political Party members.

As we've seen in the chapter "HISTORICAL ROUTE OF DEMOCRACY", the development of the "industrial revolution" and the multi-level development of the technology that it has brought to the human society in the last 150-200 years, imposed both the living and the educational level of the Working People, which is the majority in modern society.

This fact has also led to the society's remodeling by the creation of new social and income classes and has resulted in an ever-increasing popular demand for Democracy.

Among other things, this society's pressure (at the beginning of the "Industrial Revolution" era) for more Freedom from its enslavement to the upper class, forced the Monarchy, which was assembled all the political and economic power, to divest and share some of its Political and Economic power, in the created new Political and Economic elite, to save whatever it could.

So, the Monarchy slipped into Oligarchy.

- So far, we can say that human society owes today's big step forward to Oligarchy since Oligarchy finally eliminated the "Divine Monarchy".

Now, remains the next and last step of society to its Freedom and Self-determination. The step towards (real) Democracy.

This step will not be easy because Oligarchy, in order to be kept in power, has been very cleverly and effectively fortified.

Using the wealth and political power that has acquired as tools and weapons in its hands, will defend and maintain the hegemonic position it has formed in society for 150-200 years, to this day.

Instead of its direct confrontation with the Democracy, it has chosen, very wisely, the strategy of its variation/disguise as Democracy.

The Oligarchy was (and still is) aware that, if it appears with its real barbarian and horrific face, society will not tolerate it for long.

As a result, it decided to appear as a version of Democracy so that it can deceive the People that they supposedly are the one who decides.

Oligarchs do so, in order to continue to dominate on the People.

In recent years, the disguise of the Oligarchy in Democracy has (usually) been called "Representative Republic" or "Parliamentaryism".
This forgery has passed to millions of well "educated" citizens. (As it's proven they're professionally well "educated" as engineers, doctors, architects, economists, soldierly, etc, but politically absolutely uneducated)". This is because we/they have never learned what Democracy really is.
And, we/they have never learned it, because :

- On one hand, we/they are taught to children, in the school (whose circular program is made by the ruling Oligarchy) that the Political System of our country is a kind of Democracy called "Representative Republic".

- On the other hand we hear or read in all the Mass Media, 24 hours a day, 365 days a year, that "Democracy" decided this or that, the President of "Democracy" visited the President of another "Democracy", the Democratic Parliament democratically voted for that Law, Democracy "does not have a dead end", free elections will take place held with "Democratic" procedures, this month will be the celebration of Democracy, etc, etc...

Everything "is" Democratic, with every formality!
So, we're absolutely convinced that we live in a Democratic State.
We have no doubt, and therefore no concern, about it.
We've been passive voters, obedient and executors of orders, like the women and slaves in ancient Athens.
If someone challenges it, he will look like a madman.

The power of the Oligarchy, therefore, has been founded and perpetuated, based on a BIG LIE which is sustained by a vast and deep propaganda.

So, the struggle of the Democracy against the Oligarchy becomes a struggle of the Truth against the Lie, the Light against the Dark.

This is also the "Achilles heel" of the Oligarchy because the Truth has a tremendous force: five lines on a piece of paper can destroy a massive fortification of a lie which has cost many millions to construct and maintain it.

This is attempted here. The overthrow of the enormous lie that covers all human society, all over the World.
And, the arguments that prove what is Truth and what is a lie, are unbeatable, as it'll be proved here.

"Representative Republic" is not a Democratic Political System, but a typical Oligarchic one.
- This Truth is documented by the following, that make it an undoubtable fact and not just an opinion:

Here are the proofs:

We have two categories of evidence:
(A) THEORETICAL PROOFS
(B) PRACTICAL PROOFS

A. THEORETICAL PROOFS

- **1st THEORETICAL PROOF :**

The views of distinguished philosophers and thinkers on the subject are:

- ARISTOTLE (Ancient Greek Philosopher, founder of Political science 384 – 322 BC)

The election of citizens to Public axioms by vote is considered by great Aristotle as a feature of the Oligarchy.

(**Aristotle** in its "POLITIKA, δ 1294b/8-9", speaking about the election of citizens to Public axoms): *"I say   that   the draw is democratic and voting is oligarchic"*).

We see, then, how this great researcher of human nature, in his immortal work "POLITIKA", clarifies the issue of ELECTION. He states that the democratic way of choosing citizens for public axioms (eg MP) is the draw, as their election through electoral process is typical of the Oligarchy !!

- There is an exception for the axiom of "Lord General" (who is the chief/leader of Armed Forces) and the axiom of "Public Treasurer". For these axioms, voting is permitted (and was applied in ancient Athens Democracy).

We've seen (in article WHAT DEMOCRACY IS) the statements of the most important thinkers of the last three centuries : **Hobbes, Locke, Mondesquieu, Hegel, Rousseau.**

It is added three more, of our age:

- **Cornelius Castoriadis** (1922 - 1997). Important contemporary philosopher and writer of political books.

[Transcript of the speech, in Volos/Greece on 1989, entitled *"The Problems of Democracy today"*:

"I'd like to talk to you about the current problems of democracy; I am saying today's problems of democracy and not the problems of today's democracy, because democracy nowadays really does not exist anywhere.

There are liberal oligarchs in some relatively privileged countries. In these advanced and relatively liberal countries, what is the reality? They talk about democracy. The regime is, however, a completely oligarchic regime.

Of course there are the liberal aspects of this oligarchic regime, there are certain rights of people and citizens, there is a so-called free press, but if you look at who really rules, who really has the power in their hands, you will realize that even in the worst times of so-called Roman Democracy - which was never democracy, but Oligarchy - the percentage of those who have power in society, was not as small as it is today ."

And, in another intervention he writes:

"The ancients did not know the hypocritical and deceptive notion of representation of the people, as well as great philosophers did, including Rousseau (1712-1788). For the ancients, there wasn't such an issue, and the reason is obvious: When someone gives sovereignty to some specific persons, irrevocably and for a certain period (for example, five years), he has been alienated politically by himself. "

- **George Kontogiorgis** (1947 -) An outstanding and prolific intellectual of our time, Professor of Political Science in Athens Univercity "PANTEIOS", says in his (14/7/2016) speech "Aristotle and Democracy" to graduates of Thessaloniki's Univercity:

"The legally defined entity of the State holds the political system of our time as property, and society is in the position of a private individual. The representative of the political power is at the same time principal and assignee. The citizen, therefore, is an obedient to the state and not a state partner.

In the light of this, the political system of our time is neither representative nor much more democratic. Besides, either one or the other could exist, since the coexistence of both in the same state would only be a miracle.

Thus, in the Aristotle's political typology, the current political system is classified just as an "electoral" monarchy, that is the category of the very primal, monarchicly structured oligarchy.

- **Noam Chomsky** (1928 -) linguist, philosopher, cognitive scientist, historian, social critic, and political activist. (intervewed by Tom Morello, Summer, 1996.

  Qst. : In your opinion, in what sense is our society democratic?

- *NC : "As to whether it's a democracy, I don't think that there is a simple answer to that. Democracy has lots of different dimensions. I mean, basically the question is to what extent do the people have a meaningful way of developing and articulating their own ideas and putting them forward in the political arena and controlling decisions. That's the general question. Now if you look at the United States, well, in some respects that's true but in many respects it just isn't true at all.*

So for example in the political arena, first of all there is one huge segment of social and economic life which is simply excluded from public control, in law and in principle, and it's the most important part.

It has to do with what's produced and how its distributed, and so on and so forth. That's all in the hands of what amount to huge private tyrannies, of which are about as totalitarian in character as any institutions that humans have so far concocted.

Mostly their only accountability to the public is through quite limited regulatory mechanisms — I mean the whole corporate system.

And they have extraordinary power over not only what happens in the workplace but the nature of our lives, and, given their resources, over the political system.

And you can't say that they control the media, because they are the media. That's an enormous, a huge sector of life that is out of public influence and control in a manner which would have absolutely appalled someone like, say, Thomas Jefferson, who already condemned the very early stages of it that he saw and said that they would bring an end to democracy and restore the worst kind of aristocratic rule".

NOTE: Concerning Democracy, all of them refer to the drawing lots and the personal participation of all the citizens for taking decisions. None of them mention something for political parties and citizens representation.

Also the greatest philosophers and thinkers of the past four centuries, like **Thomas Hobbes, John Locke, Baruch Spinoza, Mondes-quieou, Jean-Jacques Rousseau, Hegel,** refer and explain the difference between the Democracy and the Oligarchy. (see chapter WHAT DEMOCRACY IS).

2nd THEORETICAL PROOF :

According to its definition, as we have already mentioned: "Democracy, is the Political System by which the absolute and sole sovereign of the State is its People, ie "altogether the citizens as one person" who decides freely, voluntarily and in person, by majority vote, on every issue that concerns his society".

- That is, citizens in (real) Democracy don't vote for having some persons as their representatives to whom they will pass their will to decide on every issue that concerns the society.

- In a parliamentary system, decisions on every issue that concerns society are not taken by the People itself but are taken by surrogate entities (deputies and political parties) authorized by the People to decide on behalf / instead of him, on any matter that concerns the society.

This "little difference" (that the People don't vote for each of their problems, but vote for electing those who will vote on People's behalf for every People's problem) is the specific difference of the popular vote that creates the enormous distance between the Democracy and the Oligarchy.

NOTE: Here, the supporters of "The Representative Republic" (RR) could raise objections (which, initially, would be justified) in the category that the system of RR, is not a Democracy, while they claim it is.

- According to the above definition of (real) Democracy, they can argue that, as long as the People (as absolute sovereign of society) decides or agrees to authorize some persons (deputies, senators, etc.) or other entities (political parties) to represent and decide on behalf of People's name, then, no one can blame "Representative Republic" that it isn't a Democracy.

- The allegation is acceptable, provided that what this statement says is true: "... <u>the people decide or agrees to authorize some persons</u> (deputies, senators, etc.)..."

- Of course, this authorization that "...People decide or agree to authorize some persons..." etc, comes from the Constitution

- BUT has the People voted in order to accept the Constitution of his Country / State?

- And, in particular, has the People voted for the acceptance of the Representative Democracy political System?

    If the Constitution, and in particular the acceptance of the polity of "Representative Republic", has not passed in a special referendum, what "Democratic legitimacy" does it have?

- It, actually, has no "Democratic legitimacy".

- "Representative Republic" claims that the Constitution (which RR has imposed) has "Democratic legitimacy" because it has been voted by the parties deputies. But if it hasn't been voted by the People (by specific referendum) it DOES NOT HAVE THE REQUIRED DEMOCRATIC LEGITIMACY.

- Do the People have the possibility to replace, in accordance with the Constitution of his State/Country, the "Representative Republic" with another type of Democracy (eg the real one)?

- In addition, even if the Constitution has been voted on, BUT does not allow the "sovereign" people (and not the "Representatives") to change the "Representative Republic" with another type of Democracy (ie the real one), and preserves the permanence of the "RR", then this "oversight" is evidence that this Constitution is made to perpetuate the Oligarchy that is hiding behind democratic provisions of minor importance.

Thus, everywhere one of these two conditions is not fulfilled, then "Representative Republic" has been institutionalized in the absence of the People's will.

So, It's a deceptive political system presenting people sovereign and self-reliant while they are captive under surrogate entities' decisions.

- As far as I know and after a relatively broad survey of historical data, in most Countries/States, the existing Constitutions were drafted by the political elite of each Country and not by a process of popular participation for the selection of their core principles. Also, they weren't approved by the People through specific referendums.

Therefore, for these people is absolutely true what great Plato means by the allegory "THE CAVE" in his "POLITEIA":

None is more enslaved than those who erroneously believe they are free."

3rd THEORETICAL PROOF :

According to the ancient Athenian model of Democracy, the main characteristics of this Political System, are the following:

1. The decision on any issue that may concern the society or the State (including the conferment of justice) is taken by all of its citizens and by their majority vote.

2. The "governors" of the State are revoked by the People. The majority of the People have the power, not only to appoint and to elect but also to stop their "ruling" whenever the People believe this is needed.

3. A Democracy's characteristic feature (as we have already seen) is the elevation of citizens to Public axioms by **drawing lots** among all citizens, proving the acceptance of their political equality.

"Parliamentarianism" or "Representative Republic" does not have any of these characteristics of Democracy!

- The justification, that the implementation of the Democracy in a city of 30,000 - 50.000 Athenian citizens (like Athens in the 5th century BC) cannot be applied to a State of 10, 20, 50 or 350 million citizens, is not right.

   These special and basic characteristics required for a Political System to be really Democratic , can operate (with the existing advances of Science and Technology) in large societies, as well.

   How this can be done, is analyzed in the chapter A NEW "MODUS OPERANTI" FOR REAL DEMOCRACY .

<h1 align="center">(B) PRACTICAL PROOFS</h1>

1st PRACTICAL PROOF :

We've one, among other, clear proof that the entities (political parties and deputies) that interfere with "Representative Democracy" for taking decisions under the People's name, are supposed to (but they don't) represent the so called "dominant people".

This Truth was revealed during the historical fact that was recorded in the recent History of the "Parliamentary Republic" of Greece on July 6, 2015.

It was revealed, as soon as the next day of the referendum by which the Greek People, under unusual conditions of extortion to vote YES, they voted NO with an heroic 62%, in order to terminate their financial captivity by their "lenders", that is, the International Economic Oligarchy.

Because International Oligarchy (European Union -EU, International Monetary Fund -IMF), European Central Bank -ECB, disliked this outcome, the ruling Greek Oligarchy ("government" and "opposition" together, except the extremities) came in a meeting under the President of "Democracy", and (usurping government positions which the People had been entrusted to them with the constitutional procedures and elections) decided not to accept the expression of popular sovereignty, and to transform the NO into YES with an absolute coup d'etat !!!

With this historic event, it was revealed that the "intermediate entities" of the "Representative Republic"(MP and political parties) intervening to the process for "decision taking", do not represent the sovereign people, but they represent other's will.

The masks fell and revealed the real faces hidden behind them: Parties and deputies, **they aren't assignee of the People,** as it is well written in the Constitution and as People believe, **but they're People's assignor** !!!

In addition, it was also revealed something equally scary: these acts, proving that the Country is ruled by an Oligarchy that doesn't respect the elementary Democratic principles, were tolerated and blessed by all the other "Democratic" States which co-exist with Greece in the "Democratic" "European Union".

A generalized and gigantic hypocrisy and conspiracy against the Democracy, from the ubiquitous Oligarchy, became apparent.

When the EU, in its Founding Act, doesn't accept in it States where the Democracy doesn't function perfectly, how did it accepted this coup d'etat that took place in one of its Member States without the slightest protest for the brutal abolition of the "Democratic Order"?

- But, how would they react, since they themselves caused this coup d'etat?

- The fact that these happen in Greece and not elsewhere, doesn't mean anything.

- What happened during the last 7 years n Greece, was inconceivable a few years ago. It did happen, however, through the process of subjugation of the Country to the decisions of the International Oligarchy, after the surrender of Country's sovereignty, to them. The doctrine ***"a nation is conquered either by the sword or by the debt"*** is experienced everyday and angrily by the Greek society.

- Since the Greek society, as an experimental animal, tolerates this situation in the way it has been imposed, it's certain that in any "Western" society the application of the same situation will be imposed in a similar manner. The International Oligarchy, through the management of the experiment in Greece, has gained a very useful "know-how" for the suppression of so-called Democratic societies.

2nd PRACTICAL PROOF :

Only this proof would be sufficient for the revelation and collapse of the global lie that has been set up and maintained by the ever-reigning, two-headed (political and economic) Oligarchy.

- Palpable proof that the operating System in all the countries of Representative Republic isn't Democracy, is that the "sovereign people", who consist an overwhelming majority, suffer, more or less, in order to accumulate power and wealth to some very few persons or companies.

- It can't be argued by any means of logic that in a Democratic society the majority of citizens (who are those of deciding) accept to suffer (they and their children for their entire life and for generations) in order to accumulate power and wealth for some very few persons or companies .

    It is reasonably inappropriate.

- So, it's immediately clear: what is happening (meaning the fact of enrichment of very few with the simultaneous difficulty and misery of many) it's done without the consent of these "many".

- If, however, in a society, the opinion of many is not the prevailing opinion, then this is irresistible proof that Democracy doesn't work or does not exist in this society/State/Country.

- And, if the official State, where these happen, calls itself as Democracy, this State lies lamentably.

But this is exactly what was (and still is) happening all over the world !!

In every State/Country of the "Representative Republic" arc, Parliament decides in the long run, in the absence of the people who presumably it represents, to the detriment of the People's interests and for the benefit of the Economic Elite, which is the one head of the two-head Oligarchy. The other is the Political Elite.

Accordingly, the political system that operates to the place where this "logical paradox" occurs, no matter what the label writes ("Alfa Democracy" or "Beta Democracy" or " whatever Democracy"), it is simply NOT A DEMOCRACY. End of story.

Now, how this regime is functioning and enforcing its decisions with impeccable "democratic" processes and is self-presented as Democracy, it is the centuries great deception which is uncovered in the next chapters of this manual.

With the citation of the above evidence, the position that "Representative Republic" / "Parliamentarianism", is NOT a DEMOCRACY, but it's an exemplary Oligarchy, has been sufficiently documented by both logic and historical truth, but also by philosophical and scientific analysis.

And more specifically, "Representative Republic" / "Parliamentarianism", is the Oligarchy of the Economic and Political elite, together.

On every State, the one of these two elites is supplying power to the other, within a very tightly woven grid of mutually interconnected interests, networked internationally and upgraded within the framework of economic "Globalization ".

WHY OLIGARCHY IS PRESENTING ITSELF AS DEMOCRACY?

This question is fully answered by the fantastic but absolutely realistic dialogue developed in the chapter "SYNOPSIS" , but it is worthwhile to look further, more closely why Oligarchy is self-presented as Democracy.

Just be reminded that where the Truth is varied or camouflaged or hidden, there is some fraudulent reason. This is an axiom.

- Do you imagine what would be the result, in every State/Country of the arc of "Representative Republic" if a referendum was held with the question: DEMOCRACY or OLIGARCHY?

    It goes without saying that the DEMOCRACY option would take over 90% because in the consciousness of all people it's synonymous with FREEDOM AND SELF-DETERMINATION, while OLIGARCHY is synonymous with the ENSLAVEMENT OF MANY TO A FEW.

- And, because none enslaved human or society can progress, the choice is simple.

- Oligarchy is afraid of this, easily understandable truth. That's why, NEVER in any Country/State in the arc of the "Representative Republic", will be held such referendum.

- Another important reason that Oligarchy appears as Democracy is the transfer of its, often criminal, responsibilities back to the People; we all know that in Democracy (the real one) the ultimately responsible entity is the People because it is supposed that "People decide".

Thus, Oligarchy, with its counterfeit, has also secured its acquittal from any political or economic crime it may commit, but has also secured to pass the sense of guilt to the "deciding People".

This People's "sense of guilt" is precious for Oligarchy to be able to manipulate them better, disappearing its own guilt.

THE DAMAGE FOR DEMOCRACY AND SOCIETY FROM THIS COUNTERFEIT

Of course, this counterfeit only causes harm to the concept of Democracy. The result, that is social injustice, economic deprivation of a large part of society, looting of public wealth, the sense of pessimism, alienation of fundamental principles of human existence and much more suffering that it is produced by the Oligarchy presenting itself as Democracy, is loaded upon Democracy, which by this way, is seriously devalued.

The result of this deprecation of Democracy, is the shift of a society's portion to fascism or to a dictatorship, in order "to put things back into place", as many think, foolishly.

———————————

Thus, the soil is prepared and the "yeast" (with "useful idiots") is created within the body of the People for the next phase of totalitarian occupation by the Oligarchy: it will throw down the mask of the Republic and will appear on its disgusting and barbarous face, the one of the "New Order," which, without hesitation, will impose a new Middle Ages, far worse than that we know about, from history...

———————————

DEMOCRACY, EDUCATION AND KNOWLEDGE

Democracy without knowledge and education is impossible.
Democracy is a political System that, in order to work efficiently, it needs people with critical thinking. And this needs knowledge and education for being productive.

- **Education** is the special knowledge on an object that usually is used as professional field.

- **Knowledge** of each human is the result of the general information he gets from everywhere about the way of thinking and living.

- Both of them need the right information.

- It's the State's obligation to offer Education to its People and it's the citizen's obligation to obtain wide and deep knowledge.

Regarding "right information" we have to take into account the reality we are experiencing: For informing citizens about what is happening in their environment in order to have a better knowledge is a task mostly carried out by the Mass Media.

Whether and how MM contribute to the improvement or desecration of the society, is developed in the chapter "DEMOCRACY AND MASS MEDIA".

Citizens' education is officially provided by the State, through the "official education program".
This program keeps the child sitting obligingly on a desk for about 12 years, listening to what is one thing and what is the other thing, according to the State's choices.

And, of course, by saying "Knowledge," it is not meant any kind of technical knowledge that is useful for any professional engagement.
It is understood as knowledge that makes citizens happier with their lives and useful in society.
Because,

- what does a good doctor need in society if s/he is primarily a health's cold-blooded trader?

- what does a good lawyer need in society if s/he keeps his knowledge for wealthy clients only?

- what does a good Architect need in society if s/he designs villas only for a few?

- what does a good businessman need in society if entrepreneurship and money have become an end in his/her life?

Society, therefore, before good scientists, or good professionals, needs good citizens.

How do "good citizens" work?

- When children (tomorrow's citizens) will be taught intensively, how will they respect and serve the great ideals of Freedom, Democracy, Justice, Solidarity, progress, noble emulation, love in Mother Society and in Mother Gaia.

78

- When they are not "law-abiding" by the fear of punishment, but by the pleasure of the observance of the laws that ensure the smooth operation of a supportive society of fairness, solidarity, progression, creativity, civilization, joy.

We, therefore, want an Education that will equip people since their very early age to be cultivated, creative, virtuous, righteous, fighters, contenders, solid, free, sociable.
We want a culture of education in order to produce "perfect citizens" to compose the "perfect human society and perfect State".

What is this State?

This one, in which people live happy within.
And they are happy when everyone and all of them know and appreciate the values of Freedom, Self-sufficiency, Self-determination, Democracy, Culture. Meaning that, with intensive lessons, they have learned which is the value of these concepts.

They're trained intensively and know how to defend these values with their lives.

They've been taught that the requirement of respect for each person's freedom raises the requirement of respect for each other's Freedom.

They've been taught and experienced the value of Solidarity (all for one and one for all).

They are convinced that Justice is awarded in a way that excludes injustice.

They find a way out (i e development aid) to their inclination and creativity, of all kinds: artistic, business, scientific, etc.

They are trained to recognize the value of the other person and to emulate, not to envy.

They've understood that the prize of emulation and competitiveness is not greatest material prosperity (wealth), but the gaining of greater self-respect; self-respect with its turn, leads to broader social acceptance, offers additional satisfaction and greater pleasure.

They learn that the entity of society is superior to the individuality.

They've understood that "Who I am" is superior to "How much I have"

These and many more should be the MAIN COURSES to be included into any "official education programme", imposed for 12 years on all future citizens (together with their parents) of a real Democracy.
This will shape their whole life, while professional education is only useful to a percentage of their life.

Instead, what we find (I refer to Greek reality and I wish it does not happen elsewhere) is this: the entire political elite verbally supports that Education is the No.1 duty of the State.
They swear that they are envisioning an Education that will change society for the better and, at the same time, all of them scoff at her in the most abominable way, allowing (if not designing) an "Education of lack of education".
The (majority of) teachers carrying out the Educational holy task, have altered this task to a mere civil servant job.
And these "teachers" teach, without any resistance or protest, an "Education" that produces erudite/sciolist citizens.
An "education" that ends up producing citizens/robots and parrots who simply reproduce information instead of thinking critically, able to generate new knowledge from the knowledge they get.

An "Education", which produces people supposedly democratic, without any knowledge what democracy is. They'll spend all their lives under the rules of a pseudo-democracy. And, the worst, they are taught the misguided immature and wrong school-unionism as Democracy.
An "Education" that doesn't give birth, because none falls in love with it, in order to reconcile together and to mingle his/her spiritual essence with it.

An "Education", which asks the child and the juvenile to be deprived of his/her pleasure and to read and learn what the "program" requires for entering the College or University. After all, as having reached the age of citizen/voter, s/he finds him in a society ruled by a worthless elite.

An "Education" which, in its high level and therefore particularly dangerously, allows violence as a way of achieving goals.

Under the tolerance of an unqualified supervising authority (the Ministry or Secretariat of Education) the "anti-regime" and the "anti-fascist" student, the tomorrow's social leader, imposes his views with power and fascist methods, such as the beating of his professors, when disagreeing with him, or the "locking" of the rectors of universities within their offices and other such "beautiful" acts.

I quote an interview of Thanasis Tsaknakis, an active Greek teacher and one of the few lovers of teaching :
"Many promises through time, produced very little. The issue is political.
The desired outcome, as things stand, is the creation of sciolist people who are cheap labour, not resisting, not reacting ... "

"The issue is political", he asserts.
That is political choice advantages and promotion of others interest instead of the social benefit.
And these "others" are those who want cheap laboring hands and minds that will not resist and will not react instead of minds that will resist and will react to the unfair and the evil.

Taking the above into consideration, a question arises: can this multi-annual treatment of Education from all parties that have been elected to country's government, convince a single person that it is the result of a Democratic decision and not of an Oligarchic?

A recent statement (in an interview) by Professor of Political Sciences at the "Panteion University of Athens", Mr. George Kontogiorgis, is listed:
"It is no coincidence that to all levels of education operates a purely political education, that essentially generates thousands of soldiers to serve a system that has nothing to do with Greek society. The system creates the ethos and conditions ".

And a part of a **Noam Chomsky** interview to Tom Morello (Summer 1996) :

TM: You've also written that our education system is a system of indoctrination designed to induce obedience and passivity. Explain how this works.

Noam Chomsky: *I think we all know that from our own experiences. Starting with kindergarten and first grade, the main requirement is that you do what you're told. For example if you object, if people don't, if they use their independence, if they question what they're told what to do, if they try to think for themselves and suggest that something else ought to be done, they usually get into trouble pretty quickly. It's not uniform, but try it out on your history teacher in high school, saying "I think that's a dumb assignment, I'd rather do something else." There isn't much, uh, its a rare teacher who will give even an opportunity to discuss that option. And that goes on through college and career and so on.*

There is kind of a filtering for obedience and subordination and various penalties for independence. Now, it's not that we should have chaos and people should do anything they feel like and shouldn't pay any attention to the circumstances in which your fellow students and teachers have to exist. Of course you should, but that's quite different from imposed obedience. The kind of mechanical character of a good deal of education, which is not only unnecessary but even harmful, also contributes to that".

Is it the very harsh truth of Thanasis Tsaknakis, that **"education" is guided to serve the interests of the ruling Oligarchy"**, the crushing reality?

The answer is yours, my dear reader.

DEMOCRACY AND MASS MEDIA

We saw in the homonymous chapter "What Democracy is".

Now let's have a look at what the Mass Media (MM) is and what is their relation to Democracy.

- When we talk or read about political issues, it's necessary to know the Platonic allegory (called SPELEO and meaning CAVE) used by the ancient Greek philosopher Plato (427-347 BC) in his philosophic manual "POLITEIA".

In this, he shows with simplicity some fundamentally important things about the people's behaviour in its society.

- So we need to know these very important things about the way human society operates because they apply indefinitely so far and will always apply.

To sum up, Plato in the "Cave", describes the life of a society of people living in a dark cave that has no contact with the life outside of it.

The sun (and its light) is something unknown to people living in the cave. There is neither day nor night.

- The dim light in the cave is due to the reflections of a fire that burns somewhere out and creates shadows when some (in the outside world) pass in front of the fire. These shadows are projected on a wall outside the cave, which can be seen from an opening by the inhabitants of the cave.

So for the inhabitants of the cave, the only real world outside of the cave, is the shadows that they can see moving on the wall.

If one can get through the dangerous path and get out of the cave in the out world, he initially comes to be blinded by the sunlight. Then, as soon as he begins to see and hear, he is fascinated by the colours and sounds of nature, as there is nothing of them in the cave.
When he returns to the cave and begins to tell what the real life is outside the cave, the others consider him crazy.

If he wants to motivate them to go through these dangerous paths to exit and living in the beautiful outer real world, they can even kill him who wants to put them in such a great danger for passing the dangerous path, while they are used to, happy and free in the cave's life.

From this allegory, among other things, there are two conclusions of great importance for understanding human behaviour within its society:

1. **For each one, the reality is what he perceives with his/her senses.**

2. **None is more imprisoned than the one who, erroneously, thinks he is free.**

In these two conclusions/axioms, it is based today:
  * all the modern advertising huge industry

  * the political propaganda (with Goebbels as a leading figure)

  * the society's imprisoning to the Oligarchy

––––––––––

Let's look a little closer, the first basic notion that, for us, nothing exists outside what (with our senses) we're informed that exist near or far away.

Humans get information by their senses. We hear, see, touch, smell, taste and react accordingly, in order to avoid the danger of lurking to each step and to be able to do whatever we need to. To follow the one or the other direction, to drive a car and go to work, to cook a simple meal, to climb up the Himalayas or pilot a supersonic jet.

Since we are talking about information, we must take into account the simile of the "Cave", as presented by Plato; that is, nothing exists in one's mind if not informed that there is, as this information is perceived by the senses.

- So, if an hour ago Phuket has disappeared from the map after an unprecedented earthquake and tsounami but you don't know it because you didn't hear it happening, you may buy, with pleasure, air tickets to go there.

- If for example, I have cancer, but I don't know it yet, I may plan my holidays for the coming summer and spend on them, while in fact, it is doubtful whether I'll live until then.

What exactly the five senses are for human, for society is the Mass Media (MM).

That is, the Mass Media (MM) is the sensory organs of society, in order to know what is happening around it, for reacting accordingly.

This, so important and sensitive, society's "sensory organ", should be cared for and maintained in a way that wouldn't be susceptible to the existence of any possibility of "malfunction".
The blurred perception of reality can lead the whole society, to wrong, even disastrous directions and moves.

And, of course, this, so important for society's life "sensory organ", should be an instrument incorporated in society's body, to be the body of its body, its eyes and its ears.

BUT NOT!! This so crucial for society mechanism doesn't belong to society !!!

It belongs to individuals (!!!) who own and operate it, either as owners of companies, providing information services or as political parties members, who, when they're government they can direct the public media.

We are certain, then, that society hasn't its own eyes and ears!!
Society sees and hears, according to what another mechanism conveys. A mechanism which society doesn't own and doesn't control!

- (Don't confuse the notions "Society" with "State". The State is the mechanism to control the Society's behaviour).

That is, some individuals decide what society will hear and see, in order to decide on each step of it!! Individuals who have become, under a special State's permission, holders of the right to be the society's ears and eyes!!!

They influence and shape the public opinion, FOR EVERY SINGLE OR COMPLEX THING:
- whether the consumer will buy this or the other,
- whether the voter will vote for A or B,
- whether society should stay here or go there,
- whether it should go quickly or slowly,
- whether to say YES or NO to any challenge;
- if it has to learn or not about a threat that threatens it,
- whether it must be tolerant or not in everyone "different",
- whether to make peace or war !!!
- and much more........

"Coincidentally", these individuals, who own the eyes and the ears of society, belong to this minority of citizens which consist the local and part of the international Economic elite, one of the two legs of the ruling Oligarchy. The other is the Political Elite, the political Parties' members.

So, the oligarchy that governs each Country and all the "Western" world, under the mantle of Democracy, has removed from society the ability to see and hear by itself what is happening around it.

Society (through the Mass Media) has been taught to accept as true the facts and views that this Oligarchy presents. Views that are presented as the right thing to be done.

The Economic elite/Oligarchy, the ONLY HOLDER of the MM, directs the "blind" and "deaf" society on the road they intend to, that is the road to Oligarchy's interests !!! Interests contrary to the society's interests...

What is happening in human society by this undeniable reality is the formation of a false reality in which the modern "Western" human moves like a puppet, convinced that he is free !! So it's verified once more the wise thought of great Plato: ***"No one is more enslaved than those who erroneously believe they are free."***

It is remarkable that this is done under the guise of the strictly guarded "FREEDOM OF PRESS", which has been imposed and it's protected by Political Oligarchy law.
Whose interests will the Mass Media promote, when the ownership of the MM, which requires large investments, belongs to the Economic Elite?
The People's interests or of their owners?
Does it need a deep thought for obvious reality to be understood?

It is quoted here, as a testimony of a "present witness", the following text. It is a revealing monument of realistic self-criticism by John Swindon, a former editor of the New York Times, at the retirement reception held in his honour, written on 1880.
When one of the attendees made a toast for the "INDEPENDENT PRESS", Swindon said:
"There is no such a thing in America as an independent press, unless it is out in country towns.
You are all slaves. You know it, and I know it.
There is not one of you who dares to express an honest opinion. If you expressed it, you would know beforehand that it would never appear in print.
I am paid $150 for keeping honest opinions out of the paper I am connected with. Others of you are paid similar salaries for doing similar things.

If I should allow honest opinions to be printed in one issue of my paper, I would be like Othello before twenty-four hours: my occupation would be gone.
The man who would be so foolish as to write honest opinions would be out on the street hunting for another job. The business of a New York journalist is to distort the truth, to lie outright, to pervert, to villify, to fawn at the feet of Mammon, and to sell his country and his race for his daily bread, or for what is about the same — his salary.
You know this, and I know it; and what foolery to be toasting an "Independent Press"!
We are the tools and vassals of rich men behind the scenes.
We are jumping-jacks. They pull the string and we dance.
Our time, our talents, our lives, our possibilities, are all the property of other men.
We are intellectual prostitutes."
(Wikipedia, "John Swinton")

And, **Noam Chomsky** comes after more than one century, to ascertain the continuation of the same situation :
Noam Chomsky intrvew to Tom Morello (Summer 1996) :

> **TM:** How does the mass media play in this?
>
> **NC:** *The mass media are simply part of the corporate system and their goal is roughly that of what you read in the manuals of the public relations industry, which is very frank about it.*
>
> *We have a very class conscious business community. The leaders of the public relations industry, which is the aspect of big business that is concerned with manufacturing consent, they talk quite openly about the need to "control the public mind," to "fight the everlasting battle for the minds of men," who have to be "indoctrinated with the capitalist story."*
>
> *The leading manual of the public relations industry was written back in the 1920's, incidentally by a good Roosevelt/Kennedy liberal, highly respected in Cambridge where he lived.*

The book opens by saying something like this, that the conscious and intelligent manipulation of the attitudes and behavior of the masses is the central task of the democratic system and we, the business classes, the responsible men, we have to do it. Well the mass media are just being imbued with that conception. Not just the mass media, the entertainment industry, the schools and everyone else. That's a leading and understandable doctrine on the part of the elite sector, and they do it in various ways".

The fact that the freedom of the press is a pretext so that no one can hurt the basic tool of the governing Oligarchy's propaganda, is self-evident from the fact of Mass Media ownership.

The Oligarchy's propaganda, having the "official state's education" as well as the Mass Media at its disposal, acts based on the next axiom, as well: **nothing exists for someone, beyond what s/he is informed that exists.**

Based on these two axioms (that are mentioned before in this chapter) and mastering the science of producing virtual psychoactive situations instead of psychoactive pills, the governing Oligarchy forces society to see and hear what this Oligarchy is showing and telling. So as for the society to behave in accordance with what the Oligarchy wants ...

This is all that happens in human society during the current "Age of Mandatory Illusions".

Now it makes perfect sense that the Mass Media work 24 hours a day, 7 days a week, 365 days a year.
They do so in order to establish into People's minds THE BIG LIES, that support the governing Oligarchy's power, as irrevocable truth.

THE BIG LIES, are:

1. **"Parliamentarianism" or "Representative Republic" is Democracy** (while it is an exemplary Oligarchy, as practiced wherever it exists and as documented in the chapters hereof).

2. **There is "Freedom of Press"** (while the information of the public is absolutely captivated and belongs to the economic elite/Oligarchy and its interests, which guide it accordingly).

3. **We have "Free Economy"** (while it is governed by the interests of the Multinational Companies, the Bourse and Banking Network and their ends, as we all see and experience every day).

The Mass Media, then, is the great fortress, and the heavy artillery of the Oligarchy in this war against the Truth which should not come to the surface whatsoever. If the People unveil the hidden under these big lies Truth , then it is rather certain that the Oligarchy that is based on these lies, will collapse.

Information, guided by a giant propaganda, often with fake elements, forms a false reality in which the modern "Western" humans move like puppets, absolutely convinced that they are free to act by their own will.

This reality, the propaganda's administration of psychoactive virtual situations, also explains the "irrational" behaviour of the Greek society. It explains the political choices of the society's "majority" that, according to the rules of logic, are absurd; such as the successive re-election of the same persons and parties that led the Country to the disaster ...

Here lies the reason for the absurdity, the wrong reaction or the non-reaction of society: it is due to the citizens' deprivation of true/proper information and the formation of altered thought which is achieved by:

1. Repeatedly spreading false information instead of actual ones,

2. Disorienting people from their interests and real problems,

3. Changing the meaning of meaningful words such as Democracy, freedom, Free Economy, Free Press, etc.

4. Deprecating symbols.

5. Cultivating gradual tolerance on lies.

6. Cultivating gradual tolerance to deception.

7. Creating an unseen frame of thought in which the thoughts are guided to be moved exclusively, and repeatedly. This frame prevents the listeners' / readers' thinking from getting out of it and perceive the Truth.

8. Cultivating fear for the worst to come.

Psychological experiments are known to effectively influence human behaviour.
And it is now known how these experiments became applied political practices which, over the last 40-50 years, have taken place across some States' societies.
(Naomi Klein has done a great job with her book "The Shock Doctrine" which is recommend to anyone who cares for Truth).

- At this point, it is worth mentioning something that Corn. Kastoriadis has written in "The Greek peculiarity", 2nd volume, p. 186) : *"Pornography is the production of massive sexual products, books, films, DVDs, etc., ie substitutes, for the purpose of indirect stimulation and "satisfaction" of the clients in the absence of the real erotic object. Broadly speaking, pornography in the media and politics means producing images, broadcasts, words to stimulate citizens (viewers and voters) and the resulting creation of illusions of participation in the virtual or ideological world in the absence of the real social ' and political life.*

The client, in the absence of direct participation, "does" or "participates" in his fantasy through the show, through the party, through the representative and through the elections".

Proven, therefore, the society's manipulation through Mass Media is a given and indisputable fact nowadays.
It is practised by the governing Oligarchy (presenting itself as Democracy) which, holding the Mass Media, holds the society's eyes, ears, thoughts, opinions and, finally, decisions.

DEMOCRACY AND POLITICAL PARTIES

An inherent power that exists in every act of every human entity is the self-interest, that is, the pursuit of one's personal benefit, by its acts.

- Self-interest keeps away an extremely large amount of offers that could be made by citizens to their society, as it entails depriving of each bidder from what he offers. ("If out of the 10 I have, I'll give the two, these will be missing from me").

In exactly the same way, political parties self-interest doesn't allow parties to offer to society when the content of their offer can cause damage to the party.

When a measure would displease a significant number of voters, it wouldn't be supported by the party, despite the great benefit that this measure would bring to society as a whole.

So when the Truth can harm the party, it will be concealed from society, without hesitation, whatever the cost the society will pay.

But the Truth is the only way to help society improve, as every decision or measure based on a lie is doomed to failure.

The political parties sovereignty (which is an integral part of the "Representative Republic") is (by its nature) impregnated with this self-interest which, as a political mentality and practice, ALWAYS puts the party's interest in front and above of the social benefit.

In other words, the party is the entity of implantation of self-interest, in the decision-making bodies (parliament, government) of the State.

As a result of this attitude and practice, we have the (self-confessed) accumulation of wealth and political power to the minority, to the detriment of the many, and the society's eviction, from the decision-making centers that concern it.

CAUTION !!
Self-interest (personal and parties') ceases to exist in the function of (real) Democracy, where, for every matter, the whole of the citizens decide so that individual or party's interests and aspirations cannot prevail.

In other words, the way to exclude the sovereignty of individuals and parties from making political decisions (without the adoption of prohibitive provisions, but as a result of the functioning of the Democratic procedures) is the implementation of the real Democracy where decisions are taken by all the society together.

- This arrangement excludes any intermediary (and his interests) while the personal interest (of every voter) is lost to the huge plurality of voters.

The years of political innocence, during which the parties constituted the ark of every ideology, passed irreversibly in the Greek reality. The raging wind of the "Memorandums", that have been enforced for seven and a half years in Greece since 2010, unleashed the ark of parties' ideologies (the reason of their existence) which were guarded as their eyes and revealed that there was nothing in it.

Political parties ideologies proved to be just a pretext. Costumes without content. Clothes for mascaras. It was proven that all they were cared for (and continue to care about) was to sit at the rich table of governing Power and taste (as much as they can) the tasteful goods of the plunder of public wealth.

Where all citizens believed (each one for his own ideology and his own party) that it was a fortification of Freedom, Justice, Progress, Patriotism, Political Dignity, Meritocracy, suddenly their faith was betrayed and demolished by their own party, "Left" or "Right".

94

Each thinking citizen found that the only thing that existed under the mandl of party's ideology (which was previously defended by thousands of people streaked in the streets by delighting in their beliefs about their ideas) was the despicable conquest or preservation (even with the sacrifice of their party's "soul") of the government's power.

And the party did it, not for the society to become better, but to lay (the party's "nobles") on the rug and the rich table of Power, making exactly the same (if not worse) than the previous one, its opponent ...

The question then arises: **Since nothing helps society to be separated into parties, what is the reason for their existence?**
I would say, in fact, that the parties not only offer to the society the absolutely nothing, but:

3. They graft society (exemplified by its political leadership) with lie, hypocrisy, have dealings, laziness, dark interests, deception. That is, they push society into situations that not only don't contribute to the development of the citizen and his society but also contribute to its decay and disintegration.

4. With the omnipresent and holding party sovereignty, they inactivate and kill meritocracy, while without it society is condemned to be a swamp! ...

5. With the blossoming of nepotism (a phenomenon just opposite of Democratic arrangements) they distort the meaning and the concept of Democracy, and as a result, they devalue Democracy, as το the point some citizens to support dictatorial solutions invoked by the nostalgists of dictatorship, who lately are increasing.

6. They "commoditized" Politics.
   - Commercialization occurs because the size of each party's political power is proportional to the volume (and quality) of propaganda/advertising it can exercise in order to stay (or claim a position) in government power.

The size (and quality) of party's propaganda, is a size absolutely proportional to the available money.

As the propaganda's tools (Mass Media and money) are in the hands of the Economic elite, the political party, in order to have them, "will sign Promissory Notes" payable by the plundering of a portion of the Public Wealth (which belongs to the People).

- This commercialization of politics has led it today (and not only in Greece) to be the stooge of the Economic Elite, resulting in the invisible and spineless "Empire of Money" to invade against the world society, and to enslave People with its standard cooperators, the governments of "Democratic" States; namely the leaders of some political parties.

The interference of the party in the decision-making system (and the decision's legislation) often creates dilemmas between "what the People want" and "what the party benefits", resulting (always) in the divergence of decisions, in party's favour.

We've seen before that party's behaviour is dominated by the political syndrome according to which the Party always prefers its profit (by what it hides) from the social benefit.
This syndrome is the cause of the destruction of the continually and inept looted society, locally and internationally.

But if the existence of the parties doesn't offer to the society anything more than these devastating effects, to whom does it offer?
(because someone has to benefit from parties existence, otherwise there would be no parties if no one interested in) ...

"Without fear and passion" (as we say in Greece) the only one who is seriously benefited in the existence of the parties is the two-head Oligarchy (Political and Economic elite).

- On the one hand, all the political staff who make up the various parties.
    1. Their life's level depends on the position and strength of their party in Parliament, which, in the first place, presupposes the existence of parties in the political system.

They, indeed, have every reason (and very serious, indeed) for parties existence in the political system.

- And, on the other hand, the Economic Elite, which finances the Political Elite and, the end of the day (after elections) it collects this service several times, through benevolent acts of looting the Public Wealth, that is, the People's wealth.

Thus, the interests of the Economic Elite, it is perfectly natural and logical, to be contrary to the interests of the great social majority, since its wealth derives (mainly) from the looting of public wealth belonging to society, namely citizens, the People.

Here, at this point, a very crucial question arises about the way of supporting the interests of the Economic Elite:
- How is it possible for the Economic elite to impose its interests on society, whom it shamelessly pillages and from whom (the same pillaged society) depends the ability of this elite, to pillage it?
It is recalled that the looted society is the majority, the "sovereign People" that (in real Democracy) decides.

- The Economic elite, it doesn't be afraid of the "sovereign People" that he might cut her hands?

- Or, perhaps (the Economic Elite) is aware of what the "sovereign People" is not, but he thinks he is ...

- And, what is it?

- It's the fact that the one who actually decides is not the "sovereign People", but the Political elite (the partner of the Economic elite) fortified in its Parliament.

- And when the Economic elite is the partner with the Political elite, who is deciding on behalf of the People, then the impossible becomes possible, that is, the few can impose their interests on the many (the supposed "decision takers") !!!

- This is exactly what happens in the Representative Republic!

How can the economic elite dominate the political elite?

- It is very simple: By offering to the leadership of the various parties the possibility to increasing or maintaining the political power that each party seeks.

This is simply done in the following way:
It's a common secret that the magnitude of penetration into society, the political proposal of each party, is proportional to the volume (and quality) of advertising/propaganda that can be exercised on the society's body.

- The size (and quality) of advertising / propaganda is a size quite similar to the available Money.

So, in simple words, every party needs two things:
1st) Money
2nd) Advertising/propaganda's equipment and knowledge. That is the Mass Media.

Since the Mass Media belong to the Economic Elite, to which also Money belongs (ie both prerequisites for the victory or survival of the party), this (the Economic Elite) becomes the main regulator for the distribution of political power in the system of "Representative Republic".

Indeed, the inter-party struggle (within its "System") for claiming government power gives "Representative Republic" strong elements of Democracy.

It creates (in the eyes of the People) an image of the existence of many different choices (various parties, rivalling with rhetoric) and, in fact, the ruling entity is ONE, regardless of the electoral outcome: the UNITED Political & Economic Oligarchy.

The indisputable evidence that society is constantly governed (irrespective of the election results) by this Oligarchy are deposited in the chapter IS DEMOCRACY THE "REPRESENTATIVE REPUB-LIC"?

SELF-EVIDENT CONCLUSION:
From the above, it turns out that the parties are the main component that distorts Democracy and makes it an Oligarchy in which, in fact, their existence offers the mantle of the Democracy, under which can conceivably conceal the odious and barbarous face of the Oligarchy .

Only the act of this vast (in the extent, length and depth) deception of society (the Oligarchy to be convincingly presented as Democracy) suffices to convince every thinking citizen that this deception cannot be done for the sake of society, as every cheating is made from the deceiver in order to exploit the deceived.

So, rather than discussing WHETHER OR NOT PARTIES NEED TO EXIST IN THE DEMOCRACY, propaganda assumes that they are needed, while (according to past events and reasonable thoughts) it is absolutely certain that THEY ARE NOT NEEDED, at all.

Propaganda goes beyond this truth and proceeds to perpetuate the supposed necessity of their existence by not letting the question to be presented in the public debate about whether or not parties in the Democracy are needed.

There is never mentioned even one word on the subject in the Mass Media and there is not a single minute for this crucial issue, while hours are endless in unnecessary debates among parties' marionettes; MP and journalists
Following these findings of undisputed facts, the question arises:
- Can Democracy work without parties ???

The answer is that not only can, but it is imperative, as the functioning of the parties in the decision-making bodies (Parliament, Cabinet, Government) creates only difficulties and problems (when the governing party adopts as good what the same party rejected when it was at the seats of opposition).

The final result of absurd "party's logic":

- in Greece, society is painfully experiencing the complete economic (and not only) destruction

- in the other societies where the "Representative Republic" is applied, societies experience the accumulation of wealth and political power to a minority, at the expense (and without the will) of the majority.
Of course, this is not by any meaning, Democracy

Democracy (the real) has no need for political parties to exist. On the contrary (according to the previously mentioned) it needs the absence of parties in its decision-making centers.

99

- Besides, in ancient Athens, which is the model of Democracy, no decision was taken through parties that did not even existed, even though there were social and economic classes that were totally distinct from one another.

There are ways and possibilities for implementing the exemplary operation of the Democracy, without parties in its decision-making centers, and there is no difficulty in institutionalizing them, as long as there is a possibility for expressing the relative will of the dominant People.

This possibility can be found through a dialogue of a relative gravity. It is important to be understood the need for a society's serious reflection and the development of a wide public debate on the necessity or not of parties existence at the decision-making centers.

A public debate on this issue is the most important issue because it is the biggest political fraud which is the matrix of all the problems of human society.

Below is an illustrative example of how a "Democratic Constitution" of a "Representative Democracy" (the Greek one) distorts the concept of true Democracy by placing in a suspicious manner the political parties in the Constitution.

- THE POLITICAL PARTY, in the current Constitution of Greece, IS NOT AN INSTITUTION OF THE DEMOCRACY (as the parties members support, and as their propaganda has passed through into the people's mind) IT IS NOT EVEN OBLIGATORY THE EXISTENCE OF PARTIES!...

- There is no article in the Greek Constitution that explicitly makes the party a compulsory institution of the (described in the Constitution) Democracy.

- Typically, the possibility of a party existence presents in article 29, which states: *"Greek citizens who have the right to vote can freely form and participate in political parties, whose organization and action ought to serve the free functioning".*

- That is, Greek citizens have, potentially (ie, optional) the right (they can if they so wish) to found political parties.

100

- This means that if they don't want to, they don't establish (and therefore doesn't exist) any political party.

- So the existence or absence of parties depends on the will of the citizens.

- So, something that may not exist, can't be an institution.

- Of course, it comes the Article 37.2 of the Constitution, which implies (indirectly and slantingly) the existence of Parties, saying: *"The prime minister is appointed by the party leader that has the absolute majority of seats in Parliament."*

Why, then, did the constitutional legislator not institutionalized the parties with a particular article, as an institution constitutionally obligatory?
(It should be noted that the legislator was not the People, but some politicians and Constitutionalists, supporters of the governing Oligarchy, named "Representative Republic").

- He (the Constitutional Lawmakers) did not understand that this was creating a backdoor for the Democracy's capture by the Oligarchy?

- Or was that exactly what they wanted to do ??

And I explain, what is the backdoor :
If the Party was a constitutional institution, obligatory established by a specific article in the Constitution, the internal function of this institution (the party) would be compulsorily in line with the fundamental provisions of "People's sovereignty", according to the 1st Article of Constitution.
(1st Article of Greek Constitution :

- 1.1 The form of government of Greece is that of a parliamentary republic.

- 1.2 Popular sovereignty is the foundation of government.

- 1.3 All powers derive from the People and exist for the People and the Nation; they shall be exercised as specified by the Constitution.)

Leaving the party's founding and internal functioning outside the Constitution, as a potential/optional choice of citizens (as in Article 29), allows (any) party to be organized and functioning internally in whatever way it wants, even if this is blatantly undemocratic.

And, of course, that's what is happening! That's why we have political parties of traditional political personalities and families in the country's government, even after the "political changeover" that was based on this Constitution (1975).

That's why the nepotism is blossoming in the 21st century in Greece like we should live in the courtyard of the Louvre and the Tsars !!!

And, beware of the deception's puzzle: While the current Constitution of Greece is characterized as one of the most democratic in Europe, in Greece we have the phenomenon of nepotism wholly embedded !!! (73 out of the 300 of the House of Representatives, are "family members", who form the courtyard of the three "party-dynasties" that reign in Greece the last 50 years).

Thus, while Greece has this "democratic" constitution, the Country is governed by a family-owned political Oligarchy, linked to inherent links of blood (kinship and financial crimes) with the Economic Oligarchy of the Country.

This is the result of the existence of this backdoor in the Constitution of Greece. The backdoor, from which the Oligarchy has captured the Democracy, under the mantle of which it conceals its horrible face to deceive the "sovereign" People, in order to be able to despoil the country's and society's public wealth.

- Reminder:
  What is said to happen in Greece is not only Greece, which (for the last 7 years, after the imposition of the "Memorandums") Greece is a field of experimentation of the International Oligarchy for the study and implementation of practices that will be applied to every other society of the arc of the "Representative Republic".

DEMOCRACY AND ELECTIONS

Below are the views and thoughts of a citizen who is convinced that Parliamentarianism or Representative Republic is a variation of Democracy:

- The existence of Democracy is self-evident where there are elections, since the People's will determines his future with his vote.

- Elections are the main feature and, at the same time, a proof of the democratic political system.

- But is that not so?

- Does the wise Plato refers to me when he states, **"Nobody is more enslaved than those who, erroneously, believe they are free"?**

- Do I, perhaps, erroneously think I'm free?

- Don't I vote freely, with my will, as I think?

- Since Plato said so, should I think about it a little bit more, and more carefully?

Let's look at the data:

1. The fact that for any society's decision the majority's decision prevails and is also imposed on the minority, is a democratic element; it's not disputed, as it's valid from the Democracy of ancient Athenians.

2. The fact that today, here, a vote is being held and I'm voting, is also a fact that can't be disputed.

3. It's also not disputed that electoral procedures don't allow the results to be falsified.

4. It's also undeniable fact that neither someone bribes me nor threatens me to vote for the party (and the MP) I want. I vote with my will, the party I believe that corresponds to what I want.

5. In conclusion, I don't see to mistakenly believe that I'm a free citizen who is free to vote.

- Of course, the supporters of the real (as they like to call it) Democracy, come and claim that, yes, the vote is a democratic element, but in the Democracy of the ancient Athenians, the citizens voted for every issue/problem that occurred in their society. There was no voting for the choice of citizens in public axioms.
Citizens' choice for public axioms was made by drawing lots rather than by election, as it's used nowadays in "Representative Democracy".

• Here, then, the thing starts to get confused.

In fact, the great Aristotle (on the philosophic thought of which the Western civilization was founded) comes and tells us that the democratic way of choosing citizens for public axioms is by drawing lots, while their election by vote is characteristic of the Oligarchy!

When Aristotle says something, we can not pass it like something worthless.

And to this respect, Aristotle tells us quite clearly that the election of citizens to public axioms by a vote is NOT a DEMOCRATIC characteristic but is characteristic of the Oligarchy. (Aristotle's "POLITEIA" δ 1294b 8-9). End of story.

- Has this been taught in schools, during the lesson for Democracy? Anyway, I don't remember to have had any such lesson.

- But if it hasn't been taught, and if this truth is concealed, shouldn't I ask myself: why?

- This element, however, overturns the no. (1) given of my previous view, as stated: "the vote for any decision of society is democratic". This is no valid anymore.

- No ! The vote on citizens' choice in public axioms is NOT democratic. On the contrary, it is an Oligarchic characteristic !! The democratic procedure, for the election of citizens in public axioms, is by draw. End of story.

- However, I don't want to accept an overturning of my original thinking, and I want to insist that today "Representative Republic" is a form of Democracy rather than Oligarchy. I just keep in mind what Aristotle (and not only he) says.

- Now, beyond what Aristotle says, it's undeniable that neither bribes me nor threatens me to vote for the party (and the MP) I want. I choose and I vote with my will, the party I believe corresponds to what I want. So, one can't tell me that I'm not a free citizen who decides for the future of his society.

- But I have to read again something that I read in the chapter DEMOCRACY and PARTIES and I was interested in it, but I read it tired and I didn't understand it well.

- I found it:
    1. The size of each party's political power is proportional to the volume (and quality) of advertising/propaganda it can exercise.

        - (I have to admit that this is true)
    2. The size and quality of advertising/propaganda, is a size absolutely proportional to the available Money.

        - (I must admit that this is, also, true)
    3. In simple words, every party, in order to maintain power or regain it, needs two things:

- Money
- Advertising, meaning know-how to adequately portray party's faces and party's ideas.
- (I must admit that this is, also, true).

Since the Mass Media and propaganda's know-how belong to the Economic Elite, to which Money, also, belongs (ie both the prerequisites for the party's victory), this (the Economic Elite) becomes the main regulator for the distribution of political power in the System of "Representative Republic".

In fact, the internal struggle for the party's claim to government power (done within the framework of its "Statement") gives the "Representative Republic" strong elements of democracy; this struggle, distorted properly by the propaganda, it creates into the People's eyes, an image of existence of many different choices (different parties, competing with each other) while in fact, the governing entity is ONE regardless of the electoral outcome: the SINGLE and UNITED Political & Economic Oligarchy.

Indisputable fact that many (the People) suffer, in order for this small elite to accumulate more wealth than the total of 60% - 70% of the low-income people; this is indisputable proof that society is constantly governed (irrespective of the election results) by this Oligarchy !!

This could not have happened if the real Democracy functioned, as it is irrational, the majority (the decisions making People) to decide to suffer, for enriching a few.
- Which of these is not true?

1. that the party needs money and advertising?
   - It's true.

2. that Mass Media and money are in the hands of the economic elite?
   - It's true.

3. that those who are properly promoted by MM, are elected?
   - It's true.

4. that any party (left or right-wing) taking government power follows the same basic course, so that the small economic elite accumulates more wealth than the rest 60 - 70% of the low-income people?

   * It's true.

5. That, nonetheless, in a magical way, the majority (the People) decide to suffer, for enriching some very few?

   * It's true.

What is not Truth?

   * Everything is Truth. This is the reality we live in ....

Therefore:

   * Everything is prefabricated!

My voting freedom is in my fantasy !

The only service that the "elections" accomplish is to renew (under the visible surface created to deceive the society) the legitimacy of State governance by ONE & UNITED (POLITICAL & ECONOMIC) OLIGARCHY.

   * The voter/citizen is an Oligarchy's marionette!

   * Actually, s/he is a marionette of the economic elite to which the party assigns government provisions, highways, oil distilleries, project planning, lending and other businesses. This is how they cooperate.

   * I was thinking (a while ago) that by voting, I am shaping the situation, while it is already shaped, whatever I and my fellow citizens will vote, whatever party it may be voted, whatever MP be elected !!!

   * I am a marionette of the two-head (Political & Economic) Oligarchy!!

However, the fact that we end up finding (and agreeing) that, finally, we are marionettes of others, overthrows the other thought, which I had before: *"It's undeniable fact that neither someone bribes nor threatens me to vote for the party (and the MP) I want. I vote with my will, the party I believe corresponds to what I want".*

This proven (in practice) Truth, is very clear in Greece nowadays: the citizen is a marionette of the two-head (Political & Economic) Oligarchy.

Every citizen, all over the world, in every "Representative Republic" will live this clearness, when there will be the "moment of Truth". The moment when the next move, either you (the bullfighter) will be killed by the horns of the bull or the bull will fall down from your sword.

A perfect proof of this reality (that the course of things don't depend on the People's decision and is inconsistent with it) is the historical rejection of the outcome of the Greek referendum of 5th July 2015.

That day, the Greek people (under unprecedented blackmail conditions to say YES) said NO (overwhelmingly 62%) to continuing his financial captivity to his "lenders."

The next day, and because this result was opposite of the will of the International Oligarchy, the governing Greek Oligarchy ("government" and "oppositions" together) they decided not to give expression to popular sovereignty, and to do the NO, YES !!!!

Then, they revealed the up to then, well-hidden Truth: Parties and MP, THEY ARE NOT THE PEOPLE'S ASSIGNEE (as the Democracy demands, and as it is written in the Constitution and as the People believe) but THEY ARE THE PEOPLE'S ASSIGNOR!

- (For the historical truth, it is reported that from this decision, both the extreme Right party and the extreme Left party abstained, but they didn't condemn the coup to the People).

Ultimately, it seems that some they are right to say that we live in a matrix, an illusion, scientifically designed and masterfully engineered by the governing Oligarchy, to believe that we have Democracy because elections exist.

- Plato's wisdom, once again, proves to be a great teacher and guide of our life, as, through the parable of "Cave" in his philosophical work "POLITEIA", he shows that: **No one is more enslaved than those who erroneously they think they're free.**

With elections, then, there is a perfect deception: While the People are confident that the government has been elected by their vote, what the People does (with impeccable democratic procedures) is the legalization's renewal of their mandate to the governing Oligarchy, so that it can legally take decisions on behalf of the People, regardless of the winning or losing parties in the elections.

But with the election of "Representative Republic", something else, extremely convenient for the oligarchy, is happening: The elections also function as a "Siloam's font", in which all the guilts and crimes of the governing Oligarchy are washed out and they are loaded onto People on the grounds that they, with their choices, elected the Alpha or Beta party, which, with its mistakes, brought damages or destroyed the State.

That's, the Oligarchy has so cleverly set up the game that, while it is the one that decides on everything, throws (absolutely Democratic) on the People the responsibility for Oligarchy disastrous decisions.
This has an important consequence: People feel guilty! They are convinced that (because of their decisions) they are guilty of the destruction of their society and, having blamed themselves, they acquit in their conscience the real guilt of their destruction.

And so, at the first chance (of the next elections), they revote the destructors of their lives, empowering them to repress it! ...

The persistence of a large part of society to entrust (with elections) to the proven incompetent to re-govern the Country, is interpreted by many as the inability of the People to understand what is being done to them.

However, if we accept that the People are stupid or "mass", then we condemn to death, not just Democracy, but also Logic.

And because Logic cannot be absurd (which is impossible) it must be found the cause of the unreasonable People's reaction in their political choices.

My own analysis of the phenomenon concludes that the People are exempt (for their unreasonable choices) because they act under the influence of scientifically (mainly by TV) brainwashing (equivalent to psychotropic substances) which, during the act of voting, makes them acting in confusion, with no brains, incapable of thinking logically.
And we all know that any culprit, who was in a situation of "loss of conscience" or "no-brains" during the crime, is forgiven .....

The chapter ends with **Cornelius Castoriadis:** "........ *we aren't and you aren't free, not one day in 5 years. Because what you will vote on this day in 5 years is already written. It's predetermined by the situations that these people have already created.*
From the moment when irrevocable representatives are elected, the first and foremost job of these irrepressible delegates - not to believe in Santa Claus - is how to guarantee their re-election.
Everything else is secondary, and you are currently seeing it not only at the level of delegates but at the level of the Presidency of the Government.
The only issue that is of their interest is how to guarantee re-election. Everything else, whatever teachers of Constitutional Law teach at the university and so on is, I'm sorry, nonsense."
(author's translation)

DEMOCRACY AND ECONOMY

Aristotle for Economy and Money.

From many modern economists who developed this science, its founder is considered to be the great ancient Greek philosopher Aristotle (384 - 322 BC).

Aristotle, from the 4th century BC (through his works "POLITICS" and "ETHIC NIKOMACHIA") has given us important and very useful pieces of wisdom advice, such as:
- Excessive wealth or excessive poverty creates undermining of the political stability and order.

- Neither a person nor a social class is allowed to gain excessive power.

- Equilibrium in society is ensured by a lively, educated, reasonable, strong middle class, which will achieve the counterbalance of excessive claims of limbs.

- Poverty creates preconditions for crimes and revolution.

- The accumulation of money (or goods) beyond what is necessary for a smooth (without deprivation) life of man and his society brings destructive results

- He predicted and discouraged the use of money as a commodity, ie as a product that can be sold and bought.

- He argues that the nature of money is to facilitate transactions; the commodification of money is contrary to its nature, and anything that works contrary to its nature brings devastating almost effects.

It is astonishing that if human society had listened to this great philosopher's advice at this point (that is, the mode of money's operation) we wouldn't have today all this destruction that we see both in the environment and in the human society that commits crimes for the accumulation of wealth, both at an individual and international level.

The stock market bubble of trillions, which is a multiple of the value of the whole world production of goods, and which is responsible for the bubble of social "prosperity" of a sick society living in an absurd situation within this bubble, is the result of this "out of its nature" operation of money, in our time.

———————

It is understood that in a really Democratic society, the design of its Economy is grounded in central decisions of the People.
Does this happen in "Representative Republic"?
Let's explore it :

Over the past 50 years, mankind has been living, all over the world, the confrontation of mainly two models for the economy's organization:

- "FREE ECONOMY"/ "CAPITALISM", with the Liberalism and Neo-Liberalism as its political expression

- "CENTRALLY PLANNED ECONOMY" with the Socialism and Communism/Socialism as its political expression.

After the dissolution of the Soviet Union (1989), the communist model collapsed, largely drifting the socialist model.

Whether there could be another "Central Planned Economy" model with other dosages of internal freedoms, with significant differences from the failed Communistic/Socialistic, is a debate that has no chance to be done, within the collapse of the fallen model.

Thus, the "FREE ECONOMY" prevailed to all the world.
But this economy, whose DNA is set to seek and cause the constant growth of each cell of it, begun to create ever larger cells, larger economic entities (multinational companies).
In the context of an environment of freedom without limits (that is to say, impunity) which was imposed by the Free Economy through appropriate laws, this increasing began, in the last 20-30 years (the era of "Globalization") to create giants who are eating whatever smaller exist around them.

The result of this voracity was that the giants began to eat or merge with other giants and they gave birth of monsters that began to determine the world market (and by extension, the smaller ones) according to their own programs, aspirations and interests.

These monstrous giants have become so great and powerful that they've been able to impose their will on political decisions, especially at the "big" States, which impose their will on the "smaller" ones.
So nowadays it is visible to everybody the APOCALYPSE that the "FREE ECONOMY" IS ABSOLUTELY CENTRALLY PLANNED AND DIRECTED!!

113

- The Laws for combating Cartels have been made and exist to promote the proof that there are no Cartels and there is nothing wrong with the development of these monsters, but the only they serve is to give work to some supporters of "Globalization" (usually expensively paid pens with loud scientific or journalistic names).

Luckily there is the Truth which, as a realistic reality, can not be hidden for a long time by many people.

These monstrous giants have already, to a large extent, molded the policy that they push it to legislate for their interests and against the societies interest that it is supposed to be represented by the governments of "Representative Republics".

This has made giant companies even more giant and has transformed them into a new power that wants to dominate absolutely Politics and through it, human society.

Nowadays, we are experiencing the phase that this supposedly Free Economy's abnormity, the monsters of global economic Oligarchy, has taken the dimensions of empire power; we could call it the "Empire of Money" that wants, with "Globalization" to complete the blocking of its global power over Politics, so that human society cannot lift its head again.

The demand for this dark and invisible Empire, which is developed with the "FREE ECONOMY" and the SILLY CONSUMPTION as its flags, is not the Money; It has already conquered it and it is the tool that this Empire uses to buy TOTAL DOMINATION ON SOCIETY.
Its ultimate purpose is its authority over the People's life and death (and not only).
This is what they want: To feel that they are God. With a decision of them, thousands of people could be happy or death! ...
This is the Great Evil !!!

This seeks as its final target the dark and invisible "Empire of Money" that has already acquired the characteristics of a religion.
And it will achieve its purpose if human society doesn't disarm it on time.

Already, this Great Evil, has gone through most of its way and is preparing to complete it, through the Economic Globalization which this dark power organizes and develops for its world domination.

At this point, is very appropriate the reference to the Greek poet ODYSSEAS (ULYSSES) ELYTIS, when at a press conference given on October 19, 1979, at the "Great Britain" hotel of Athens, on the occasion of his award of the Nobel Prize for Literature, he said:

"I already told you. *It's barbarism.*

I see it coming masqueraded under lawless alliances and prede-termined enslavements.

It may not be about Hitler's furnaces, but about the methodical and quasi-scientific subjugation of Man. His absolute humiliation. His disgrace.

So one wonders: What do we fight all night and day in our workshops?

We are struggling for nothing, but it is everything.

They're the democratic institutions, which all show that they'll not endure for long.

It is the quality that none gives a penny for it.

It is the entity of the individual, who goes towards its total eclipse.

It is the independence of small nations, which has already become a dead letter.

It is ignorance and darkness. That the so-called "practical people" - mostly the current bourgeoisie - mock us, is characteristic.
They see nothing. We see everything. Where is the truth, it will prove one day when we will not be here anymore.

115

It will be, however, if will be worth the work of one of us all. And that will save the honor of all of us - and of our time".

(author's translation)

- Instead of presenting other evidences for the above categories, I quote an article of mine, in which there are the most important proofs relatively the real situation of the relations between Democracy and Economy.

This article was published in various blogs in Greece, on 18 / XI / 2016 under the title : **"Globalization of Democracy or Oligarchy"?**

"On the occasion of the outgoing US President Barack O'Bama to visit Athens and Berlin, as well as the recent election of Donald Trump as the new US President, and also the pressure on the EU to sign the CETA treaty, two concepts have been heavier in the public debate: **Globalization** and **Democracy;** in both Athens and Berlin, most of what has been said concerned these two concepts on the lips of "high" guests and hosts, as well as in the TV panels of politicians and journalists who are usually invited.

At some point, the existence of one (the Democracy) depended on the success of the other (Globalization).
It was said (by the outgoing US President, if I am not mistaken) that the prerequisite for the existence of Democracy in ALL THE WORLD is the success of the attempted Economic Globalization.

And, of course, when from a huge airplane descends a huge and shimmering Barack O'bama, he climbs up and in front of an audience in tears from its admiration for the speaker, he talks to you about the good of the Democracy, and about the best that Globalization brings, with what kind of stature can Othon Iakovidis speak of, descending from the always late, dirty and stuffed trolley, without tearful listeners, without (not even) a step to speak ?

However, the Truth has divine qualities and can appear at any moment from everywhere, with incredible power, which stems from the common logic; it can overturn every situation and every lie, as good as it is, no matter how convincing it is and no matter if it is coming from the most formal lips, even those of US President or Frau Merkel, the "Gauleiter" of European Union, who both of them, made a duet to teach us what good things Democracy and Globalization are for human society ....

116

But, Frau Merkel forgot to remind us that, according to the Democracy's Principles she believes in and which she is leading in Germany and EU, she took off her panties and she was pissing contemptuously and defiantly denounced the Democratic result of a People's Referendum (the Greeks that she admires "because they gave birth to Democracy").

Since then, she has imposed her will on this People, in an extortionary manner, that has no relation to the Democracy, which she blatantly and detestably affects, as she imposes her will on a "Greek" government of marionettes which imposes the reversal of the result of the Greek Referendum of July 5, 2015, becoming from then a dictatorship, in the face of her eyes !!

So, in practice, Frau Merkel has proven irrefutably that what she means as Democracy has nothing to do with Democracy.

So, when she talks about Democracy, she means something else from what the name and definition of Democracy mean.

Mister President (Barack O'Bama) has also forgotten to mention some of the key achievements of the United States Democracy that advertise globally as a model of Democracy, but also as a global guarantor of it.
Bellow they are quoted a few, which happened during his 8-year-long US presidency and forgot to say:
1) Billionaires in the US, over the past 8 years, have risen from 359 to around 600.
The wealth of the 400 richest of them (according to Forbes data for 2014) skyrocketed from $ 1,100 billion to $ 2,290 billion !!!
During the same period, US workers saw more than 7 million jobs lost and more than 5 million homes were seized by banks that had, in the meantime, been subsidized by the US state (ie taxpayers' pockets) with more than $ 3,300 billion.

2) According to the 2010 figures for every new American billionaire born of O' Bama' policy, there were 130,000 redundant US workers ...

3) the number of homeless children literally living on the streets in the US exceeds 1 million ...

4th) In 2009, at the start of the 2008 crisis and at its most painful moment, according to the Fortune American magazine and the famous Fortune 500 list, the 500 largest US monopolies increased their profits by 335% !!!
These groups, in the immediate future, saw their profit reaching 391 billion dollars.
The fact is a real feat if it is taken into account that it is the second biggest gain in the list of "Fortune 500" in its 56-year history!

6. Note 1: In the year when they increased their profits by 335%, the same groups proceeded with the dismissal of 821,000 workers.

7. Note 2: According to the Rockefeller Foundation, one in five US workers in 2009 had income losses of at least 25%.

8. Note 3: Today, the average American household has an income below 2000 levels, with per capita GDP steadily declining for four decades.

6. Note 4: About 55 million Americans (according to the National Academy of Sciences) are living below the poverty line, of which 15.5 million are children. That is, with about 100 million, 1/3 of the American population, they face severe economic distress.

7. Note 5: Over 50 million Americans don't have health insurance and 50 million are fed with food vouchers.

8. Note 6: Joseph Stiglitz records that 95% of the profits generated by the O'Bama model from 2009 to 2012 in the US have resulted in the richest 1% of the population, and Paul Krugman notes that of these profits 60% went to the tycoons of wealth that account for just 0.1% of the population.

(all the above mentioned figures were copied from the article "Ku Klux Trump" of the reputable journalist Nikos Bogiopoulos in "The PressProject" of 12/9/2016, translated by the author).

When these are the results of Democracy then, what would the Oligarchy or the Monarchy need, in order for the rich to become richest?

So: what President O'Bama calls Democracy is not Democracy, but Oligarchy, for the simple reason that many cannot decide to be miserable for enrich a very few (the Economic elite).

"FREE ECONOMY", therefore, proves to be ABSOLUTELY GUIDED BY THE ECONOMIC ELITE that dictates its will in the political system, so that it legitimizes (by impeccable democratic processes) its over-enrichment.

This Truth is so simple and so documented that neither 100 O'Bama and 300 Merkel can dispute it !!!

So we see clearly that Frau Merkel and Mister O'Bama when they talk and say that globalization is necessary to establish "Democracy" in the world, they mean as Democracy, the disguised as Democracy, Oligarchy!

However, (cannot be done otherwise) the Oligarchy's actions, reveal its identity and the Truth !!! .....

The grand motto of the globalization's edifice is "FREE ECONOMY".
We are all aware of its results that shapes the fact that "FREE ECONOMY" is as free as the very few multinational corpora-tions that control it all over the world, permit:

- **Energy** (BP, Chevron, Shell, Exxon-Mobil, TOTAL, etc.)

- **Food** (MONSANTO, NESTLE, UNI-LEVER, ETC.)

- **Water** (VEOLIA, SUEZ, AGBAR, RWE, SAUR, ETC.)

- **Medicines** (BAVER, ABBOT, GLAXOSMITHKLINE, PFIZER, etc)

- **Information** (MICROSOFT, GOOGLE, APPLE, FACEBOOK)

- **Military equipment** (DASSAULT, GENERAL DYNA-MIC, FERROSTAAL etc.)

119

- **Money distribution of** (FEDERAL RESERVE, GOLDMAN SACHS, CITIGROUP, MORGAN STANLEY, PARIBAS, DEUTCHE BANK, ETC. THROUGH A NETWORK OF CENTRAL BANKS AND STOCK EXCHANGES).

So, the very popular "FREE ECONOMY", not only ISN'T FREE but it is ABSOLUTELY GOVERNED AND GUIDED by the Economic Oligarchy !!!

Human society without real Democracy is doomed to move with an economy that is the chains of its enslavement to its dark masters hidden behind the mask of the Democracy.

Directions are given to societies through the organizations developed by the Oligarchy of these multinationals so that they can only be seen by the results that few read or perceive their significance.
These organizations are:

- **World Trade Organization WTO**

- **Organization for Economic Co-operation and Development - OECD**

- **International Monetary Fund - IMF**

- **World Bank - WB**

- **Bank for International Settlements – BIS**

These institutions, in order to pass their decisions to the governments of the States to make laws that compel societies to obey them, are coordinated with decisions taken by other bodies, informal but stronger of these organizations, such as:
- **the Trilateral,**

- **the Bildenberg Club,**

- **the Summit of 20 (G20)**

In this way, Globalization is tightening human societies more closely to the interests of this Money Oligarchy; we must say, IT DOESN'T TARGET AT THE MONEY, since it fully owns the production and distribution of it as it pleases them.

120

Money is its weapon to conquer its ultimate purpose, which is THE FULL SUBJECTION OF HUMANITY to their will.

Things are very dangerous because, from supporters of the so-called "Democracy", like O'Bama and Merkel, we are led to a new "Dark Ages" era of most terrible barbarity, from the old we know.

Thus, those who feel FREE PEOPLE WHO CAN'T AFFORD THE ENSLAVEMENT TO A BARBARIAN ELITE, they are obliged to fight it.

The only way to prevent the evil that is coming galloping, is to RE-ESTABLISH THE REAL DEMOCRACY; thus it will be ripped from its foundations, the edifice which is founded on a big lie".

Through this article, we've seen what the situation and relationship between "Democracy" and "Economy" is in the society of US that is the model of Democracy.
What is happening outside the US to enrich the richest at the expense of the poorest does not have to say a lot.

It's enough to see the wilderness of the ruined cities of the Middle East (and not only) and the caravans with miserable human beings as refugees who desperately leave their houses and all their belongings and walk or swim to the unknown future.

This is the result of growth within and outside the Countries in which this Economy who is presented as "free" while is fully bound to the interests of the "Empire of Money".

DEMOCRACY IN THE 21ST CENTURY

PROPOSAL
FOR A NEW "MODUS OPERANTI"
FOR (REAL) DEMOCRACY

- **George Oikonomou** ("Direct Democracy" p. 109): *"The imagination that highlights our will in the invisible future is the human capacity to face the future, as memory is the instrument of the past."*

- **Corn. Kastoriadis** ("Weather", pp. Epsilon, p. 100): *"The political imagination has disappeared. This disappearance of the imagination goes along with the collapse of the will. Because, to be able to want something it doesn't exist, you must be able to bring it into your mind. And, in order to be able to imagine something other than simple repetition, you have to want it in all of your heart".*

The following proposal describes an imaginary Democracy function that has all the characteristics of true democracy, as the Ancient Athenians taught us and as modern human needs and can have it.

- Do we need another Democracy than this we live in?

This question concerns (at least) all of us who are living in Countries/States which are ruled by the Political System of "Representative Republic" or "Parliamentarianism".

After all that is written in the previous chapters of this manual, it comes as an undeniable answer :

No, we don't need another Democracy.

WE NEED THE REAL DEMOCRACY!

The one that we have seen and defined in the chapter "WHAT DEMOCRACY IS " of this manual.

And, we need the (real) Democracy, not for theoretical reasons, but for three very practical ones:

1. To enable every citizen to have a truly enjoyable life; with freedom, protection and lack of deprivation, so that s/he can develop his/her skills and creative concerns in a friendly, safe and enjoyable social environment.

2. Because the tangible results of 200 years of society's governance from the falsified Democracy of "Representative Republic", all over the world, are now known and obvious to anyone who knows writing and reading; results that are at the expense of the overwhelming majority of society, which is exposed in the appetites and decisions of a small minority that has found the treacherous way to govern.

3. In order to prevent a very small minority from mocking and deceiving us, our family and all the society.

- **Can we do this? And, how?**

The only way for this to be done is if we, the People, govern ourselves and don't allow to be ruled from other entities.
That's what Real Democracy does. Society is moving according to its own decisions, and not according to the decisions of a particular very small minority that subdues the People and governs over it.

So how does the (real) Democracy work, so people can be governed by themselves?

- Self-evident answer: The People must be the one who decides on every issue that concerns him.

Can (and how) People take decisions on every issue
that concerns him?
Is there a way to do this in practice?

- This is the fundamental question that, if answered with a proposal feasible to implement and convincing of its effectiveness, will provide a very big step to the restoration of the true democracy to mankind.

So, together, we will first explore this hub and, if a convincing answer is given to the question, we will then proceed to finalize the proposal for a model of real Democracy for the 21st century.

Things are as follows:
The main objection of Oligarchy's supporters to the implementation of the real Democracy is based on two main points:

1. In the claim that it is practically inapplicable to have referendums very often because of the cost, but also because of the availability of each citizen, every two or three days to be called upon to decide on issues they don't know and perhaps they don't care about.

2. In the claim that the Democracy's model of ancient Athens (40.000-60,000 citizens who were gathering in one place to decide and vote) cannot function in our time due to the large size of the modern State (of 10, 40, 50 or 150 million citizens) and its extensive geographic area within they live.

The Oligarchy's supporters they're right in these very critical points for three main reasons:
1. the concentration of millions of citizens in one place is not feasible

125

2. the high cost of a referendum,

3. every citizen cannot have the view and willingness to reflect on all the issues that concern the State and have to be resolved almost every day.

- Can we overcome these obstacles?

Let's see:
- Supporters of regular referendums with the help of electronic voting offer a solution to the problem of meeting all the citizens of the state in one place (in the same online ballot), as well as to the problem of the cost of a referendum.

- They don't, however, solve the other problem mentioned above: in that every citizen cannot be called very often, almost daily (not having knowledge and opinion on all the serious issues that require a solution) to decide on their settlement.

- The modern science of electronic networking can offer a lot to the (real) democracy, but not to frequent, almost weekly, decision-making.

- This is because the question of a national decision affecting thousands of citizens is not so much the technical part of the vote (which is being solved with the existing technology) but the qualitative part, concerning the substance on the issue of the decision. That is the mental preparation of those who decide on a decision that will affect the lives of thousands, or millions of people. This requires knowledge of, often multi-sided and complex, subjects.

- Every citizen can't, every day, be engaged in the study of serious problems of any nature (from Sanitary and Environmental, to Economic and National Defense), in order to decide in practice.

He has his jobs, the stress of every day's life and his problems, which don't allow him to act additionally , at the same time, on a daily basis, as a conscientious "MP".

The solution to the above problem is offered by the science of Mathematics and Statistics.

- In our age, the science of Statistics has found (and has proven) that a small, randomly selected (according to this science) subset of an entire population decides in the same (quantitative) way as it decides the total.

- for example, if we ask a referendum question, and the result records eg 55% NO and 45% YES to 10 million voters and the same question is put to a total of 500 - 600 citizens randomly selected according to the rules of statistical science, we will have almost the same result: 55% NO and 45% YES.

- This is a reality, theoretically founded and practically proven for decades now. It is the base for the huge advertising industry, as well as for the policy that guides the course of important areas of our lives, as it is today the great helper in the research field of all sciences, from Medicine to Astronomy.

- Up to this reality, and to the results provided by statistics, huge amounts are invested daily across the globe.

- This fact (the opinion's identification of the many, with a small subset of them) leads us to think that we can have 500-600 citizens (randomly selected according to the rules of Statistics) who will be permanently and exclusively employed to studying and deciding accordingly on issues that today (in the "Representative Republic") the elected deputies vote in a hurry and according to the line of the party, without knowing what they are voting, as they themselves admit.

- Thus, **we can have a House (a Parliament) whose will, will be the primal will of the whole People,** and not the will of third parties/intermediate entities, that allow the genuine People's will to be distorted.

The unquestionable effectiveness of Statistics, which is scientifically substantiated, offers to (real) Democracy a surprising possibility: to overcome the difficulty of regularly meeting ALL of one country's citizens in one place, in order to make decisions on every issue that concerns their society and the State.
Science ensures the right choice of the proportion of the participants (accordingly their economic situation, origin, place of residence, occupation, etc.) so that the decision actually reflects the people's will rather than the interests of a faction that has become in a position of strength.

In this way, we can have a Parliament that can, on a daily basis, take absolutely democratic decisions, just like Referendum.
Decisions that will have the democratic quality and equal value of a referendum.

- The functioning of this Parliament will not, of course, abolish the classic Referendums, by a vote of all the citizens of the country, on matters of major importance.

So: This subset (of 500-600 citizens for a population of 10 mil.) may well, as a HOUSE OF PEOPLE'S WILL, validly echo the society's opinion :

- to legislate,

- to control the executive power/government (from which it will be completely independent).

128

For the time that these randomly selected citizens will be "MPs" (let's say one year), they'll have devoted all their time to legislative work and government control, which (government) will be completely different corp, entirely independent of Parliament/House of People's will.

Thus, having no other employment, they will have the time it takes to gain the basic knowledge of each and every issue that emerges in order to decide in a responsible way. Their detailed information, of course, will also be assisted by the Scientific Committees of the House, covering every area of knowledge.

CAUTION: The (eg 600) citizens who make up the Parliament are NOT REPRESENTATIVES of the People. THEY ARE THE PEOPLE HIMSELF.

The will of this Parliament's majority is not the will of the Parliament; IT IS THE WILL OF THE MAJORITY OF THE WHOLE PEOPLE.

This is confirmed by the science of mathematics and statistics.

This is a way in which society itself can express its will directly, just as a referendum of all the citizens of a State would be.

So, the objection of those who don't want real Democracy on the pretext that the model of ancient Athens cannot function in modern States due to size differences (60,000 inhabitants vs some million inhabitants), is forfeited.

This arrangement (the Parliament to be constituted from selected by draw citizens) brings about two radical changes, as:

1. **The election procedure for the selection of deputies is abolished;** it's replaced by the draw of the deputies among all citizens.

- It is also repeated here that the great Aristotle in his "POLITICS" declares and teaches us that "…. *drawing is the democratic way of choosing the citizens in the public axioms and not their election by vote, which is a method of the Oligarchy.*"

2. The presence of political parties in Parliament is abolished.

- Regarding to the need of the parties existence for the functioning of the Democracy, there is an extensive reference to the chapter "POLITICAL PARTIES AND DEMOCRACY".

- So: Common sense dictates that there is no reason to continue to feed a parasite to drink our blood.

  - The parties will remain as political organizations of reflection, cultivation and expression of political positions, ideas, theories and opinions. They simply will not have any role in decision-taking procedure.

These two reforms, namely, the abolition of the parties presence in the Parliament and the abolition of the electoral process for deputies, bring, without the need for any legislative prohibition, the listed below beneficial effects :

1. We have a Parliament (Legislative and Audit Authority) with truly free opinion and will, completely independent of the Executive Authority, meaning the Government.

- This independence is necessary, in order for the Legislative and Audit Authority to be able to impartially control the Government and to legislate fairly, outside and away from all sorts of party's feats, duties or obligations; there sometimes hide the economic aspirations of third parties outside the House but directly associated with the parties.

2. **The Parliament ceases to be an organ of the ruling party** as it is today (as is the case today in Greece) because it must stop the unacceptable present phenomenon, where the auditor (Parliament) and the auditee (Government) are the same person (the Governing Party). This, in addition to abolishing effective control, violates the Constitution itself by abolishing the imposed independence between the three Powers (Legislative - Executive - Justice).

- eg the Constitution (of Greece) allows and legitimizes the concentration of all powers on the Prime Minister's seat. That is, with impeccable democratic procedures, legitimizes the NON DISCRIMINATION OF THE THREE POWERS of the Republic (Legislative, Executive, Justice) !!!

- This is what the Greek people is paying today (with his enslavement in the "Memorandum") even though it hasn't been perceived by all.

3. **Political commercialization,** that is to say, the election of persons in the State's axioms, in terms of marketable products **is definitively abolished.** This also abolishes the opacity and corruption that, in current election practice (all over where the "Representative Republic" is functioning) the dependence of the MP and the party is hanging on the sponsor's generosity for the advertising campaign.

4. **The umbilical cord, through which the Mass Media power** (and its bosses Oligarchy) **can manipulate political power, is finally and irrevocably cut off.**

- Thus, **the possibility of a substantial transfer of political power that is now being made from Politics to Money, is finally and irrevocably cut off.** This transaction between Politics and Money predetermines the persons who make up the eligible civilian personnel, making the electoral process a simple statute of finalization of an election that has already been made (before the elections) by newspapers and television screens.

5. **The "CUSTOMERS SYSTEM", which makes the citizen "client" of the ever ruling party, is definitely and irrevocably abolished.**

   - (this "system" is responsible for much of the current corruption and disaster in Greek society).

   - The citizen is permanently relieved of the position of the obliged to the Party for promoted him to favorable positions.

   - Thus, citizens will regain their lost political and personal dignity.

6. **It is definitively open the (closed, today) road to meritocracy,** without which it is impossible to have progress and development in any field, social or privet.

   - Thus, the productive capacities of society (especially of young people) which are now trapped, will be liberated.

   - Automatically it is definitively abolished any possibility of nepotism continuation

7. **The bonds of Justice with governmental and party power are finally and irrevocably dissolved,** and so the way for a truly independent Justice opens.

All of these benefits for the society are achieved by only one reform:

* **the selection of the deputies by drawing lots instead of electing them by vote; simply, automatically, without a prohibitive legislation to be imposed; ONLY through ONE (but fundamental) CONSTITUTIONAL REFORM.**

THIS IS THE ONLY REFORM NEEDED TO TURN THE POLITICAL SYSTEM OF "REPRESENTATIVE REPUBLIC" FROM OLIGARCHY TO DEMOCRACY.

We see, therefore, that the benefits that society derives from changing the way in which deputies are elected are of enormous importance.

Probably (and naturally) some of them may not apply to some societies.
But what applies with this settlement to all societies operating as "Representative Republic", is that:

1. It will be impossible to any small minority to mock and deceive all society.

2. It will be possible for each citizen to have a truly enjoyable life. With freedom, protection, help and lack of deprivation, so that can develop skills and find answers to all creative concerns.

Since we have a way of setting the People at the decision-making center and making People real and not supposedly dominant, let's see how the whole structure of a political system of real Democracy could be shaped.

A NEW FUNCTIONING MODEL
FOR REAL DEMOCRACY IN THE 21ST CENTURY.

In relation to the above mentioned principles and elements, this is the way that the real Democracy could function in the three Demmocratic Powers: LEGISLATIVE POWER - EXECUTIVE POWER - JUSTICE.

A. LEGISLATIVE POWER
(HOUSE OF PEOPLE'S WILL / PARLIAMENT)

- HOUSE OF PEOPLE'S WILL / PARLIAMENT, consists of a specific number of citizens to be selected by drawing lots among all citizens of the State.
    1. the exact number will be derived from a relevant study for each State. It will be about 500-600 citizens per 10 mil. population.
    2. their age limits, other possible specifications, the manner and procedure of drawing lots of citizens/deputies, will be decided in such a way that there will be no question of its transparency.

- Deputies will offer, against a parliamentary fee to be decided (without incurring retirement costs) the normal services that a Deputy offers, ie control on acts or omissions of the Government and voting or rejection of the laws to be brought by the Government or by a group of Deputies for voting.

- Special Scientific Committees of the Parliament, for each subject and field, will provide their knowledge and opinion, so that each Deputy before his vote on a matter will be aware of the necessary elements of the matter.

- Before taking up their duties, Deputies will spend a fast-track (eg 2 months) seminar for their national importance duties.

- The Bureau of the Parliament will be composed of top judges, also chosen by a draw between them at regular intervals; they'll haven't the right to vote for decisions to be taken by the Parliament.

- The same will be the case with the Presidencies for the Parliamentary Thematic Congresses.

Such a composition of the Parliament, in addition to the above-mentioned advantages:

1. **Abolishes the existence of a political elite.**

    - The Parties sovereignty ceases to have reason to exist.

    - (in Greece, this sovereignty plunged the Country into swamp and destruction)

2. **It cuts off every possibility of the Economic Elite invading the political process.**

    - It eliminates the excessive government funding of the parties, since they will no longer face huge election expenses, which also create financial dependencies.

B. EXECUTIVE POWER (Government)

1. It is exercised by the President of the Democracy, who is elected by vote directly by the People for (say) 4 or 5 years.

2. He can be recalled by the House of People's will, under special circumstances.

3. He forms the Government from persons of his own choice, from (presumably) distinguished on each field, citizens.

135

- The government's composition will be of the absolute choice (and responsibility) of the President of the Republic, who will select his Ministers among citizens of Greek nationality.

- It is self-evident that the government will be made up of the best in each sector, citizens

- The assumption of the duties of each one of them must also have Parliament's approval.

- The way of nominating candidates for the Presidency, the process of this election, the specifications of the candidates and so on, are secondary elements which will be finalized after relative public dialogue and consultations.

- The re-election of the same person, in the presidency of the Democracy, will be allowed once.

- The President of the Democracy (as well as all the Minister's decisions) will be accountable to the Parliament.

- (Details, will be settled after and through a relative public dialogue and consultations)

C. JUSTISE

- With the removal of Political Parties from parliament, Justice automatically acquires independence.

- The control of justice will be carried out by the Parliament, that is the People himself.

- The jury will be strengthened. JUSTICE WILL BE EXERCISED BY JURY COURT, in which the judges will only preside over the procedure, and the decisions will be taken by the jurymen. (A system similar to the USA).

Here finished the outline describing the way in which the real Democracy can operate in the 21st century.
It is understood that, as an outline, it may certainly need corrections.

The proposed here model of operation for a real Democracy at the core of its conceive, contains the fundamental characteristics of the real Democracy as they appeared and functioned in ancient Athens:

1. Decisions on every issue are taken directly from the People on all the issues concerning the society
2. The public offices are given by drawing lots (among all citizens)
3. Election for the President (executive Power) by the People's vote
4. No intermediaries in the decision-making bodies,
5. Revocation of the selected executives
6. Independence between the three Authorities (Legislative, Executive, Justice)

A genuine democracy ought not to allow, but to pursue for ensure the participation of all.

Aristotle, in his "POLITICS", writes: ***"Democracy's characteristic is the guiding principle for everyone to decide on all issues without exception, as this equality is pursued by the people."***

GLOBALIZATION
OF THE (REAL) DEMOCRACY

An idea, in very general terms:

As long as we have accepted the rationale that the expression of a people of 10 million citizens is taken from the verdict of only 600 citizens, appropriately selected according to the rules of the statistical science, then we can conclude that the verdict of 6.000 of citizens expresses the decision of a people of 100 million citizens, or the verdict of 9,000 citizens expresses the decision of a people of 150 million citizens, and the verdict of 18,000 citizens expresses the decision of a people of 300 million citizens.

- That is, the "HOUSE OF PEOPLE'S WILL", the real Democracy's "PARLIAMENT" which is described in the chapter "A NEW MODEL OF REAL DEMOCRACY" can be applied in every state, however large its population is.

Of course, when the number of citizens for the Parliament is numbered by some thousands of citizens, it should:

- provide for their common residence in a village or town (specially built for this purpose) for the duration of their term.

- Provide for the use of electronic voting, telematic "meetings", and any appropriate technological facility, both for their comprehensive specific information on any topic they are consulted and for the expression of their verdict.

139

- Assuming that all these technical problems can be solved (and they can, indeed) then a global political will is needed so that humanity be able (by replacing or complementing the UN) acquire a "HOUSE OF GLOBAL WILL", a "GLOBAL PARLIAMENT".

- It will consist of 450,000 citizens (so many they are count proportionally to 7 billion inhabitants of the Earth).

The number of Deputies from each Country of the World will be according to its population.

Deputies will stay for the entire duration of their term (say 6 to 8 months) in this city that will be built exclusively for the residence and the mission of these people. (Greece, as the birthplace of Democracy, would be the ideal place for the place for the "HOUSE OF GLOBAL WILL".

- The only thing the Deputies of the "GLOBAL PARLIAMENT" will have to do, will be continuous monitoring (from a specially organized information system to provide them with objective information) of every international issue they are asked to vote on.

- Their decisions will be mandatory for a "GLOBAL GOVERNMENT" which could consist of a 5-member "SECRETARIAT" (one from each of the continents) who could be elected by the "World Parliament", among the celebrities honoured with the Nobel Prize.

- From the "Global Parliament", a "Cabinet" will also be elected.
  1. Perhaps the UN, with the experience it has acquired in International networking of countries, can play an important role in this global governance.

- And, of course, in such a settlement for a global government, global referendums should also be included.

Everyone realizes that with such a Global really Democratic Parliament and Government, humanity will always be exempt with wars (local or general), poverty, illiteracy, environmental pollution, the threat of nuclear havoc, and every evil that threatens it today.

140

Global society does not ask for anything more.
What we ask for is feasible and the road is one: The Real Democracy.

The way to get to such a World Democratic Parliament and Government is simple but not easy: everyone to work for establishing the (real) Democracy to his/her Country.
That's the first target .

EPILOGUE

"Manual" (*"encheiridion"* in Greek) means "a small book of elementary knowledge of a science or an art, but also a kind of small knife, dagger".

So, I can safely say to you, dear reader, that this very moment you are holding in your hands a small book/dagger that can help, on one hand, the revelation and on the other hand the stabbing of a monster. A monster which, like a modern Minotaur, requires to consume continuously ours and our children's present and future, and has already consumed much of it.

This "manual" was not written to add something to the philosophy of political science or the theoretical substance of the (real) Democracy.
 I don't seek to present myself, as a teacher or as a thinker.

I, simply, ascertained, through my last ten years of struggle for real Democracy in Greece, the need for a tool that would effectively help the interactive confrontation with opposites to Democracy or differently thinking citizens.

If Democracy does not win the fight primarily on the field of ideological controversy, it's impossible to win it on the practice field.

Taking advantage of the relative quietness offered by the retirement age and the reluctance of Greek society to revolt - even peacefully - against its current captivity, I tried to manufacture a tool that can facilitate the struggle in this crucial field.

What I, hopefully, have made in this manual, is a clear look at events that often times go unnoticed by the many; it is also an analysis and classification of the basic elements and parameters of the theme "Democracy", which every supporter and fighter needs to know, so that s/he can successfully cope within any discussion about Democracy with anyone.

So, this manual was written, for two very practical reasons:

1) To become a tool in the hands of people struggling to support the Truth of Democracy, without themselves having a broad view and deep knowledge on the subject

- (Let's not lose sight of the fact that we all run exhaustively to catch the consumption's "carrot"; there is no time available or constant appetite for "searching the Truth").

2) This manual can be proven more useful, however, to open up conservative views of citizens who are unsuspected about how some others disable their judgment capacity and exploit their potential. These citizens that their existence causes the great Plato to shout with all the power of his wisdom and soul: ***No one is more enslaved than those who erroneously believe they are free.***

And, it is not at all derogatory to have a wrong opinion in good faith.
It is derogatory for somebody to stay stuck and stumble in the darkness when s/he holds candle and matches on his/her hands.

Whether this "manual/dagger" is properly forged, lightweight in hand, sharp and bright as a candle, it'll be judged by all of you who will use it.

Finishing this manual, it comes again into my mind, what the excellent highbrow Cornelius Castoriadis, writes:

- *"We need this constant creative activity of the public and this means, above all, the passion for the public, for the common Freedom. If there is no such passion for the common, we can say good speeches, we can write fine books, construct systems that are impeccable, philosophical and political, but they will not mean anything if they'll not become specific acts".*

So, in order not to let things hang in the void, it's suggested, using this manual to create a Global Network of Real Democracy Supporters.

As a first step in creating this Network, a FaceBook Page titled WE NEED REAL DEMOCRACY is already existed.

If there is a reasonable turnout, this FB Page will evolve into a "Site" in order to become a tool suitable for the initial organization of a World Movement.

Any reader of this manual who agrees with the need for creation of a great international political force, outside the known paths of political parties logic, makes the first step and becomes a "friend" on this FB Page.
That's all !

> But even for those who do not wish to use this facebook page there is always an open invitation for collaboration and communication by any means.

Next steps will be found and decided by all of us together, there or anywhere.

And, we must never forget the Thoukididis lesson:

**_"You can have either FREEDOM or QUIETNESS.
Both, together, don't coexist.
You have to choose:
Either you'll be FREE, OR QUIET "_**

——————— · ———————